DO MEN SUFFER?

WHY DO MEN SUFFER?

Books by

LESLIE D. WEATHERHEAD

THAT IMMORTAL SEA

THE RESURRECTION AND THE LIFE

PSYCHOLOGY, RELIGION AND HEALING (Rev.)

WHEN THE LAMP FLICKERS

THE SIGNIFICANCE OF SILENCE

A PLAIN MAN LOOKS AT THE CROSS

THE WILL OF GOD

IN QUEST OF A KINGDOM

PERSONALITIES OF THE PASSION

THIS IS THE VICTORY

WHY DO MEN SUFFER?

PSYCHOLOGY AND LIFE

HIS LIFE AND OURS

AFTER DEATH

JESUS AND OURSELVES

THE TRANSFORMING FRIENDSHIP

WHY DO MEN SUFFER?

LESLIE D. WEATHERHEAD

Call the World, if you please, "the Vale of Soul Making." Then you will find out the use of the world.

—*The Letters of John Keats*

ABINGDON PRESS
NEW YORK • NASHVILLE

WHY DO MEN SUFFER?

L

SET UP, PRINTED, AND BOUND BY THE PARTHENON PRESS, AT NASHVILLE, TENNESSEE, UNITED STATES OF AMERICA

DEDICATED

In unfading remembrance

to

ELIZABETH MARY WEATHERHEAD

my Mother,

and to

MURIEL WEATHERHEAD

my Sister,

whose bodies were defeated in the battle against painful disease; but who, from that defeat, wrested a spiritual victory which challenged and inspired all who knew them, and made glad the heart of God. And to all proud sufferers who, with broken body and unbroken spirit, are seeking to achieve for themselves and for others

The Conquest of Suffering

CONTENTS

PREFACE

To strip away all mystery from life would be undesirable, even if it were possible. Mystery is essential to worship. The being of God must soar up into infinitude, far beyond all power of human thought and imagination. A God whose ways could all be comprehended by so insignificant a creature as man, would be a God inadequate for such a universe as this. We cannot even understand his universes—for we are told there are many—and "these are but the outskirts of his ways. And how small a whisper do we hear of him! But the thunder of his power who can understand?"[1] It is perhaps childish to want to unveil the mysteries. It may be better to say with the psalmist:

> "The Lord reigneth; let the earth rejoice;
> Let the multitude of isles be glad.
> Clouds and darkness are round about him:
> Righteousness and judgment are the foundation of his throne."[2]

In one sense such a conclusion is the conclusion of this book. Yet an effort will be made to peer into the darkness, and to make sure that some of the clouds are not within the minds of men rather than around the throne of God.

The subject of Pain has haunted my thinking ever since I began to think for myself at all. My mind has

[1] Job 26. 14.
[2] Psalm 97. 1-2.

followed every gleam which promised light on so dark a problem. I have written, and torn up, and rewritten. I have studied and pondered and prayed. I have been helped by conversations with those who can think more clearly and who can see further than I can. Every minister is brought almost daily into touch with some phase of human suffering and feels he must have some *progressive* hypothesis about it.

So I release this book. Its vision is as much as I can see after twenty years' thinking, though I long for fuller light. I can only hope that some who have not had time or opportunity for much thinking may find help, and that those who can see further and more clearly may be led to share the vision which God has shown them.

It is impossible to thank adequately all who have helped me. My beloved father-in-law, the Rev. Arthur Triggs, has not only corrected the proofs, but he has offered, from the rich treasures of his mind and heart, suggestions which have been eagerly adopted. The Rev. Hugh Martin, M.A., has corrected the proofs and made valuable suggestions. Once again I am greatly indebted to all that my wife has done in the preparation of this book. Footnotes show as much as footnotes can of my indebtedness. None of those to whom I have applied for permission to quote has denied me. Both Miss E. M. Bailey and Mr. Philip Found deserve special praise for doing so efficiently the dull and detailed work necessary to the production of a book.

Yet my chief indebtedness is to a host of men and women who have suffered and who have given me the rich privilege of their confidence.

As I have sat by their bedsides I have seen the gleam

of a golden secret which they carry forever in their hearts. They cannot tell it completely, for it cannot be said in words. But, far better than the theorists, they know that somehow pain and sorrow are caught up into God's heart and carried there; that even agony is both redemptive and redeemed, and the heartbreak of the world becomes music.

They cannot solve the mystery of pain. The strangely moving thing about the greatest sufferers I have been privileged to know is that they never use the word "mystery." To them pain doesn't deny God's love and power. Suffering does not mock him. They know that somehow it has been met and dealt with and is being redeemed. It is awful, but spiritually it cannot hurt them. They can bear it because they can bear the thought of it. Life's song was in a major, and is now in a minor key, but it is still music, and they listen not as those who are affronted or resentful, but as those who understand. All bitterness has gone.

. . . And in my dream I stood with an angel on one of the balconies of heaven. And the angel allowed me to lean over and listen. But I could not bear to hear. Sounds of pain came up to me: the cries of widows, children in agony, strong men wounded and mutilated, the burden of the bereaved, the lonely, the bewildered, the frightened. Men crushed women beneath their feet, and starved little children, and hunted their brothers into poverty and unemployment and disease. Even women hurt one another with cruel deeds and malicious words. There were pains of body and mind and soul, which no one on earth could understand and no one could cure. The world seemed full of sorrow and pain, and the sound of it all came up to heaven until my soul was sick.

"How can God bear it?" I cried. I felt angry and frightened and in despair. "How can he dwell here in serenity when the sound of man's anguish, in unbroken crying, lifts itself to heaven? What means this endless moan of pain?"

In my dream the angel turned to me a face which I cannot describe. There was pain in it such as I had never seen in a face before. Yet there was joy too outshining it. There were tears in his eyes. Yet through the tears a triumph shone. And he spoke to me. When he spoke, I knew that there was not a pang of pain on earth that was not shared in heaven. More, I knew that what men suffered on earth was only a faint reflection of the anguish God and his holy angels endured on man's behalf in heaven. Somehow it came to me that through all its pain, which he more than shared, God with man was working out the world's redemption, and that there was no other way; that, in a sense, the endless moan of man's pain was the song of a world being redeemed, a sad song as yet, but still music, working toward some worthy and wondrous climax beyond all human capability of thought.

The angel spoke to me again. But when, at the sound of his voice, I lifted my face, I could not bear to see the anguish in his eyes. Nor could I understand his words. Yet a great peace enfolded me; a vast, calm silence wrapped me round. I slept.

When I awakened, the sun was shining through my windows. And God's peace was with me still.

L. D. W.

Leeds, England.

CHAPTER I

SOME ASSUMPTIONS

It must be said, at once, that this book does not attempt to offer a glib and easy answer to problems which have baffled so many earnest and able thinkers. Even after centuries of thinking the problem can be stated in ways for which, as yet, we have no complete answer. I do not write because I can give an answer. I write in the hope that those who read may see that there *is* an answer, even though no words can fully express it, nor mind yet apprehend it. The very vastness of the problem has tended to reticence in the writing of books upon it. If the publication of this one seems presumptuous, my only defense is that scarcely a man or woman gets to the age of forty without being troubled by the problem of suffering, and to leave the problem entirely alone, because it is too big for us to solve completely, is to withhold help that can be offered.

Every working minister who is in touch with the needs of men and women, knows how they torture their minds by aspects of the problem of suffering to which no tabloid reply can be made. Yet much could be said to ease the torture and the mental pain if one had the time and if the sufferer were in the mood to listen. When suffering comes, however, neither time nor mood is right. One can only grip the hand and offer sympathy. This book attempts to drop an anchor firmly before a storm begins.

I am, personally, very deeply distressed to notice to

what small extent members of our churches have thought their way through the problems of Providence. Recently, even a minister, who, of course, should be a leader in religious thinking, wrung his hands at the bedside of a friend of mine who was dying of cancer, and said, "I do not know why a good man like you should be allowed to suffer thus." The patient had progressed far beyond such a point of view. To him, his suffering was his share of the burden of the world's suffering, the suffering which came from the ignorance, folly, or sin of the great human family, which God did not will, but which he allowed him to help carry in partnership with himself. To my friend the world had gone wrong. Suffering was part of that wrongness. And God had asked him to join a great team who were trying to get that wrongness right.

So this book goes out, not as an exhaustive theological treatise which presumptuously supposes that an age-long problem is solved in its pages, but merely as the message of a preacher who is troubled to discover that so many fine men and women add to their sufferings a torture of mind which he believes comes from bad thinking; a preacher who believes that his message does not fail to face the stern fact of suffering, but is one which, from this angle or that, can throw light on that fact, and help people to face it bravely, bear it nobly, and contemplate its existence without thinking that it denies either the goodness or the power of God, while, at the same time, fighting with the utmost power against the tyrannous sway of suffering over the minds and bodies of God's children.

Some people have the greatest difficulty in believing that

there is a loving, powerful Intelligence behind the universe. So many things go wrong, so many disasters happen, that they have given up believing in God altogether. Others remind me of the poem of Walter de la Mare, "The Listeners." They wonder if there is "Anybody there" at all. As they travel through the world they knock on its doors and beat on its walls. But no one comes to answer that knock, and they turn away sadly. For them there is no one there. That question, "Is there Anybody there?" is one of the most important a religious man can ask. However vast Jeans and Eddington and others prove the universe to be, it is still, in a sense, a prison from which man cannot escape, at any rate while in the body. Man, with all his knowledge, still hammers on the walls of his prison and wants to know if there is Anyone outside; whether he is somehow caught as a rat in a trap and can understand nothing, or whether his life is in the hands of Someone very wise and very good, who ultimately will successfully work out a scheme, a purpose, in which the life of the individual man plays a part and in the light of the whole of which all his suffering will be justified.

Just lately we have all been horrified by calamity upon calamity. We opened our papers one day and read that an English ship had gone down with all hands. Two days earlier we found that two hundred of our fellows had perished in a coal mine. Two days before that we read about a railway disaster. A few days earlier than that we read about a burning liner. Two days earlier still we read about a typhoon that had swept thousands of our Japanese fellows into another life. And there must be scores of people, who, through personal calamity, family bereavement, and paralyzing sorrow, have lifted up their hands in anguish, crying with great poignancy, "Is there Anybody there?" Or is life meaningless, its happenings just accidents, so that nothing means anything at all?

I found an illustration a little while ago that helped me very much. My children sometimes play with a cardboard box in which there are a number of pieces of card, and on each card a letter of the alphabet. If I should take a handful of those letters and fling them in the air, they would fall down on the floor and we should regard it as very strange if even two of them came down in such a way as to make a little word of two letters. If we should go away and in time come back and find one word, however short, and *however chaotic the other letters seemed to be,* we should say: "This looks like an evidence of mind. Somebody has arranged the letters thus." If we should go away and come back and find not only words but sentences, and not only sentences but an essay, *even if we could not understand all the words that were used,* we should say, "This *is* an evidence of mind." If we should take a box in which were a number of little pieces of card, and on each little piece a note of music, and fling it up into the air, then go away, and on our return find that the notes made chords, or that a number of the notes as they lay there made a melody, let alone a harmony, let alone a fugue, we should say: "A musician has been here. This is the mark of a musical mind." We should *know* that a purpose was being worked out, even if sometimes it sounded as though there were a discord; even if some of the music seemed to jar and be out of tune.

I have myself found comfort in the fact that though there are very many words in the universe that I cannot understand and cannot interpret, I am quite sure that the universe is a word, a sentence, an essay, a theme, and not just a number of incidents flung out haphazard. I have found a comfort in the faith that believes the universe is harmony, even though there seems to be discord in it; the faith that believes the universe is a fugue in which a theme is worked out with variations. I cannot always follow the way the fugue is being interpreted, but definitely it *is* a fugue, so that even when it is in a minor key it remains music, and I should know it to be music if I were musical enough.

The alternative, as I think we must admit, is incredible. The alternative asks more of credulity than the Christian interpretation of the universe asks of faith. The alternative means that Mendelssohn's music, and Shakespeare's poetry, and Turner's pictures, and the song of the lark, and the moan of the violin, and the glory of the dawn, and the scent of a rose, and the pageantry we call the sunset, and the majesty of the stars, and a woman's love, and a little child's laughter; a great deed, a noble life, a sacrificial act, and Christ on his cross, mean no more than the scum on the sea, no more than the water in which we washed up the tea-things. That is incredible. It is impossible. It makes a madhouse of the universe.

It is very impressive, is it not, that wherever we put our finger down in the universe, we find that the truth discovered in one realm of inquiry fits in with truth discovered elsewhere? In other words, here is a specialist working in his own area who discovers something which he is convinced is the truth. Here is a scientist working in a different area, and he finds something which he believes to be the truth. Think of the two discoveries as notes of music and you find that when you play the two notes together, there is a chord. When you put the syllables together, there is a word. There is purpose, there is design, there is a mind, there is a heart. To take a very simple illustration: You work in one area of investigation and try to understand the life of the bee. You work in another and try to understand the life of the flower. Nobody can deny that the body of the bee *means* flowers; that the structure of the flower *means,* implies, what cannot be understood without the bee. Together they make a word. Together they make a chord. So it is with these things that seem to be discord, meaningless, irrelevant. They are only so because we cannot yet read all the words; we cannot hear all the harmonies. You go out some evening, and you are moved to the very depths of your being by the glory of the sunset. Your dog looks at it but he is not moved. It is because there is not only the pageantry of beauty. There is your response as well. It would be true to say there is no beauty existent in the sky alone. It is equally within the mind of the perceiver. There is a link between that beauty and you who perceive it to be beauty. Two syllables—beauty and appreciation; but put them together and they make a word.

Of course anyone may think I am spinning a theory out of touch with terrible facts; that I am just sentimentalizing about sunsets and dawns and flowers. "What of the other side of life?" they say. "What about its calamities and troubles that make us ask within ourselves whether there can be Anybody there?" Let us face that. I can take you to a home where there is a mad baby. Of course you may say that it is an exception. Most babies are born mentally normal. You may say it is a eugenic problem. I know; but what are you going to say to the mother of that baby? Are you going to talk to her about sunsets and birds, when her little one lies on her knee insane? I can take you to a home from which a man, aged nineteen, went out concerning whom tremendous things were prophesied. He was going to the university, but, instead, he went to France. During the Great War, on the second day he was in France, he was blinded in both eyes, and he has been in pain ever since. "Is there Anybody there?" It is a question his father has ceased to ask. I can take you to a friend of mine, who worked for years to make a business, and built up a magnificent organization which gave work to many. Then, at the age of sixty, he took into partnership a man who was a knave, and who brought the whole thing crashing down on them both; and now my friend, at sixty, is looking for a job. I can tell you of a woman sent to me by a doctor. He wrote a note and she brought it to me. He said: "This woman has got into the hands of a fiend. He forced her eight times to an abortionist and then he deserted her. I have tried to patch up her body. Can you do anything for her mind?" I can see her sitting in my room with her eyes bright with that awful glitter of the disillusioned, her mouth just a thin line, and when I talked to her about a God of love, she said, "I don't believe you." Why should she? "Is there Anybody there?" I think of a man, unemployed, down and out. He had just one joy in life, and that was his little son, aged ten, a little chap in whose life the father lived. A week or two ago the boy stepped off the curb and a motor knocked him down and killed him. "Is there Anybody there?" Has the universe got out of control and run amok? Is life all meaningless and its pain a horrible accident?

I believe I could take each one of these cases quoted above and show why it was allowed to happen, and how it fits into the scheme of things, and sketch out a Christian philosophy of the universe that includes them all and explains them. This will be my purpose in the pages that follow; but in the meantime look at some other illustrations.

I have two friends who went out to the East as missionaries, both of them well educated, a man and his wife. After they had been married fourteen years, God gave them a little girl, and they entered into a happiness they had never believed existed. One day the little girl was playing among the flowers in a tropical garden with the sunlight in her hair. The next day she was lying dead. You can imagine that bungalow with the windows darkened, and in that inner room the man and his wife standing by the side of the coffin in which lay their little girl and all their hopes. The man said to his wife, "One day we shall see God in this too." "If we are going to lose her," he had said, as she lay dying, "we won't have her snatched from us like this. We will offer her back to God." They didn't believe that God had sent their sorrow. It had come to them out of the ignorance of the universe—some disease we have not yet learned how to fight or prevent. But they saw in their anguish God's challenge, and they knew that if they co-operated with God, they could turn the agony into a sacrament. So they refused their furlough. They would not even seem to run away. There are deep lines in the man's face, but a deeper note in his preaching, and the woman's hair went whiter, but the radiance never left her eyes; those two are still in the East witnessing for God, because they *believe* there is Someone there. They make better sense of the universe than an atheist does.

On July 17, 1927, a local preacher was addressing an open-air meeting in Bristol. He was trying to make the point that Christ is the answer to all our problems, and the solution of all our troubles—rather a difficult thing to prove; rather an easy thing to say. He was saying it with great personal conviction. Then a great fellow at the back began to heckle, and shouted out: "Shut up that d——— nonsense. What do you mean by talking to us like that? Don't you realize that economic laws govern the situation, and Christ has nothing to do with it? That is just the kind of stuff you people talk. That's the way you bluff people. Go and talk to the unemployed like that, and see what they say." There was no answer, until a man very near the front stood out and said: "I am not used to speaking, but I can answer that. I am unemployed, and I am very poor, and I have a wife and three children, but if you take Jesus Christ out of my life, I have nothing left. He is greater than my poverty, and I love him." That last sentence is one of the finest things I have ever heard of. There was a time for questions, but no questions were asked. People went quietly home. "He is greater than my poverty"—the sentence left nothing else to be said.

Do not misunderstand this. Do not suppose that this is the church's answer to unemployment. Far from it. It is a terrible thing, which the church and every other organization have got to fight to the death. But the glory of Christianity is that, in the meantime, whether or not a man understands such explanations as I want to put before the reader in this book, he can triumph over the desolating things that come to him. He does not think God sends them. He does not see God's intention in them. It is not God's will that men should be unemployed, and live in slums, that they should be exploited, and be victims of industrial tyrannies; that they should suffer agony through disease and pain, through fear and worry. That unemployed man saw that if he lifted up his trouble to God, in co-operation with God, he could make out of his trouble something beautiful, something sacramental, something lovely, because he believed there was "Someone there" to whom every life was precious and who would never let him go.

Three assumptions will be made in this book.

The first is that there is such a being as God, a creative, infinite Mind who brought this universe into being and who continues to sustain its existence; a Being, moreover, who is at least personal. By this I mean, that since personality is the richest possession of the human being, God must at least be personal. He may be suprapersonal, that is, having abilities of which we know nothing, a far richer nature than the word "personality" usually connotes. A much bigger word even than personality may be needed, could we guess the truth. But he cannot be less than personal.

The second assumption is that God is good. Of course it is open to people to claim that God is evil, that somehow a malignant Fiend has found his way onto the throne of the universe. If this be true, then I suppose it could be argued that man's suffering is a logical result. It would even be looked upon as part of the torture which the created must expect from the creator, or as an accident in a badly made universe; an accident in which God has no interest or concern. The fact that no serious thinker has ever held this position is for ordinary people sufficient guarantee that it is untenable. Since we are bound, by our own sense of values, to think that kindness is better than cruelty, and love better than hate, the supposition that God is cruel would mean that man is a higher being than God: would mean, in other words, that the stream had risen higher than its source—an impossibility of thought.[1]

The third assumption we shall make is that God is omnipotent. The first chapter will ask what we mean when we make this claim, and will try to discuss in what senses God has power, and in what senses he is temporarily defeated. We feel, then, that our reply to J. S. Mill's famous dilemma, in regard to the world's suffering, that either God is good and not powerful, or else powerful and not good,[2] must make two points clear. God is good, but we need to understand, much more fully than we have done, what goodness is: that it is not, for instance, the rather weak indulgence of a father who spoils his children. And, secondly, that God is all-powerful, but that we need a far wider understanding of the nature of power. But I make here the assumption of God's omnipotence, meaning that, ultimately, God can achieve his own divine purpose in spite of, and even through, suffering, and that although God can be, *for*

[1] As Doctor Grensted said in his Bampton Lecture for 1930, "This awareness of the good as good has absolute, a compulsive character, which completely resists analysis. We can compare goods, standardize them, schematize them, but the fact of value, worth, goodness is, in itself, final and irreducible." *Psychology and God.* L. W. Grensted, p. 12 (Longmans, Green & Co.).

[2] The argument ran that if God were powerful enough and good, he would prevent suffering. Since it exists he cannot be both. Either he allows it because he is not good or because he can't help it.

the time being, thwarted, frustrated, evaded and defeated, he can neither be put off the scent and be made to give up his plans for us, nor can his purposes be *ultimately* defeated by the forces which seem to be arrayed against him. It is absurd to suppose that the purposes of One worth calling by the august name of God can be hopelessly and finally defeated, say by the ravages of germs which are part of his own creation, or by coal falling on the body of a miner, a fall which is an expression of one of God's own laws.

Further, it had better be stated at once that the author believes that the final answer to all the problems of suffering is the answer of faith. It is a faith very strongly supported by intellectual discoveries, as we shall see. But the picture in the author's mind is that, at one point, it is as though the hard ground of reason were cleft by a narrow gorge on the other side of which is the certainty about God to which he would like to bring his readers. By running across the hard ground of fact he believes his readers would be able to leap the gorge and reach the certainty; but in all honesty he feels he must tell them, at the beginning, that the hard ground will not carry them all the way. It will support them so far, and then it will demand a leap of faith. He hopes that men and women will read the book before the agony of some great calamity is upon them. It is so difficult, in the midst of the agony, for the mind to examine arguments. It tends, in our tense hours of anguish, to run down the channels cut out for it by our previous thinking. Many a man, in an hour of calamity, dimly and fatalistically accepts his trouble as the will of God, or blindly supposes it is punishment for sin, or resents it in bitter rebellion against God, just because he has never thought the matter out in those quiet and cool moments when the mind is prepared to break new ground and blaze out another track through this dark jungle.

The man who inquires into the problem of suffering may be compared with one who, from some sunny street, steps into the comparative gloom of a vast cathedral. After the blaze outside all seems dark, yet, as he moves forward, he finds that it is not nearly so dark as he had first thought. It is not so much that his eyes grow accustomed to the darkness, though that is part of the truth. It is, rather, that here and there are unsuspected windows which throw light upon the way he treads. There may be gloom left in the corners. There may be patches of darkness which his most steadfast gaze cannot pierce, but at the end of thorough investigation, though there may not be the sunshine of the outer world, there is no darkness deep enough to make him afraid. If he is shut in, he is shut in with God, and at the far end of the cathedral, even if his problem is not solved, it will be lifted to high places where all human resentment is answered, where suffering is defeated, for he will find that holy symbol which shows God in the Beloved Son, himself nailed to a cross of pain.

If for some to whom has come physical agony, crushing calamity, or desolating sorrow, a darkness almost tangible, in which the mind seems stunned and the spirit broken, there shines from these pages a light to lighten that darkness, healing to soothe those wounds, and courage to face that situation and turn its apparent liability into a glorious asset of the soul, then the writer will feel that his book has not been written in vain.

CHAPTER II

IS GOD OMNIPOTENT?

THE question we are asking in this chapter is this: If God is omnipotent, why doesn't he prevent suffering? One is bound to believe that if God is God at all, he is all-powerful; but what exactly does omnipotence mean? This must be our first inquiry. My definition is as follows:

The omnipotence of God is his ability to do those things which are normal functions of his power and which are in harmony with his character.

I think we need to remember that a lot of people still hold a childish conception of God, as if he were a kind of conjurer or magician. They have a sneaking idea that if God really gave himself to it, he could turn a pumpkin into a palace, and back again into a pumpkin in ten seconds, or make a round square, or express one third in decimals. Men become impatient with us if we say that there is anything God cannot do; but he cannot do that which is not a normal function of reasonable power. Yet they will go on believing that he can do things which are as absurd as those mentioned above. God cannot deny himself. He is a perfect Personality and he cannot, by the exercise of one function, do that which would contradict another. In other words, he cannot do anything absurd, stupid, self-contradictory, or out of harmony with perfect reason and perfect character. One might define omnipotence, if the reader prefers it, as ability finally to consummate those purposes which his nature and character suggest.

The revelation of his nature shows what seem to be limitations of his power in two ways: first, in the realm where human free will operates, and secondly, in the realm where human ignorance, folly, or sin, holds up his plans. We shall discuss these matters more in detail later, but it must be remembered that these limitations God has himself imposed. He *chose* that we should have free will and the power to misuse it. He *planned* that we should learn slowly and correct our folly and sin by our experience. This is not to deny his power, for we must remember that self-imposed limitations are an expression of power, and not a denial of it. God, whose will is perfect and loving, would not have imposed such apparent limitations if his purposes were to be ultimately defeated by them. Briefly, in the first case, it is his purpose to have a human free agent, not a human automaton; therefore he must give free will. And, secondly, it is his purpose to deny his purposes until man can co-operate with him for their consummation and goal. If God were less than he is in power and wisdom, he dare not create a universe with so many self-imposed limitations in it; with so many arguments to be used by us in evidence against him. It is just because he is omnipotent that those things which seem to deny his omnipotence are allowed to happen. God's power, expressed as some would have it, would end man's resourcefulness altogether. It is part of his infinite patience and love, but equally part of the revelation of the nature of his power, that he so depends on man.

We can see how true this is by considering for a moment the alternative. If God can and will do things for man which man can do for himself, then it would be a far easier solution to life to leave it to him to do. Why send for a doctor and utilize his skill? If God wants to heal a person, surely he can do it. Why pray for another? If God wants to comfort him, surely he can do it. Why take our message across the seas and lose some of our best men and women by tropical disease? Surely, if God wants to evangelize the world, he can do it. Why go and comfort the broken-hearted when God can do it? We see the fallacy at once. God cannot do it. And where it isn't done people suffer, all because of that fundamental reason that God, to educate his race, stands by, refusing to interfere even though his restraint costs him the price of Calvary.

Two things emerge from this: first, the awfulness of responsibility; and, secondly, the glory of co-operation.

A man can say "No" to God, and God is helpless to coerce, because God has given man a free will, and having given, will never take it back again. There is a sense in which God is helpless to make a man into a saint. If by my misuse of my free will I continually say "No" to him, I can bring upon myself utter ruin; and though God can use forces which are calculated to influence me, he cannot coerce me. He cannot deny himself and become the burglar of my soul. He can wield tremendous forces through the prayers of others, through the words of others, through the lives of others, through the deeds of others, through the beauty of nature, or the glory of music, or the face of a little child, but he must always stop short of divine interference. And it is only because he does this that every advance is *our* advance, every decision is *our* decision, every choice of the higher, as every choice of the lower, is *our* choice. Only in this way can we grow and develop, only in this way can we become children of God. If God were less than he is, we should be machines.

One of the most glorious thoughts in the world is, surely, that God depends on us to get his will done—that there are some things he literally cannot do apart from ourselves. When he wants something done in the world, he does not mobilize his angels; he will bring two people together, not by force, but by the winsomeness of love, and they will have a baby who will become a Moses or an Isaiah, a Luther or a Wesley, an Augustine or a Livingstone. If he wants to comfort some broken heart, he will put it into your heart to go and say kindly words for him. If he wants some inspiring message to reach an individual or a nation, out of the depths of his limitation, he will cry, "Whom shall we send and who will go for us?" And he is indeed defeated unless one shall rise and say, "Here am I, send me." It is amazing how the eternal, omnipotent God has so condescended to co-operate with man that apart from man he is helpless fully to reveal his nature or to accomplish his purpose.

Many people find it a real difficulty to believe in the power of God in relation to human life. They have no difficulty in the power of God as it is expressed in physical terms in the universe. Indeed, it would be a queer sort of mind which could fail to be impressed by the evidence of some immense and gigantic power at work, if even a glimpse of the universe is got through the eyes of a modern scientist like Sir James Jeans. Listen to Sir James describing a model of the universe: "The earth goes six hundred million miles round the sun every year. Let this distance be represented by a pinhead one sixteenth of an inch in diameter. On this scale the sun is a minute speck of dust one three thousand four hundredth part of an inch in diameter and the earth too small to be visible in the most powerful microscope. Even on such a scale the nearest star is two hundred and twenty-five yards away. To include all that we can see with a telescope the model must stretch four million miles in every direction."

We hardly need the scientist to convince us of God's power in nature. The rushing waterfall, the tearing wind, the angry wave, the furious storm, the flashing lightning, all speak to us of terrific energies in the world about us. If, as we believe, there is a God, a Master of all these mighty forces, he must have a power which makes the human mind reel and stagger.

What we find so difficult is to believe that God's power in human lives is anything like on the same scale. I want us to see that the energy that is expressed in a power that can hold the planets in their courses has its counterpart in a power that is at work in human lives. This latter point is just what people fail to see. They admit God's power in terms of the physical and deny it in the realm of the spiritual. At least, if it is not definitely denied, it is certainly not definitely believed in. We sing hymns about it much as children whistle to keep their courage up when they are walking along a dark road; but we are not nearly so impressed by it; we do not rely on it or trust in it or turn to it with any sense of reality when we need it. One of the greatest disappointments of a minister is to see a man, brought up in the Christian faith, challenged by some catastrophe, who not only finds no help in religion but never *expects* to find help in it, going, at once, to those resources which are the property of every pagan, and proving, at once, that all that his lips have said about the power of God are words which have no basis in reality.

If our minds are really to find security so that they can rest, and remain at rest whatever happens, they must *possess* the truth about God's power. I mean that our minds must not merely assent to, but believe that we are in the hands of a loving omnipotent Being who, whatever happens to us, can finally, in co-operation with ourselves, make our lives perfectly fulfill his plan.

No mere assent will do. Assent is like the music of the band to the soldier. It makes him lift his feet and keep his head up and his shoulders back, and makes him sing. But woe to that soldier who *depends* on the music of the band. When the battle begins the music dies away. Belief is a sword in the hand of the soldier. It is something he has acquired, but it has become part of him and he can fight with it, and win through by means of it.

Our belief in the power of God to win through to the fulfillment of his purposes in spite of, and through, whatever happens to us, must be a precious possession from which no tribulation can part us. Then we shall realize one of the greatest truths in the world: that what happens to us doesn't matter vitally. The only thing that matters is what happens *in* us. The only thing that matters is our reaction to what happens to us. For nothing can happen to us which has any power of its own, either to smash us or to defeat God's purposes finally.

Now, the power manifested in the universe ought to comfort us, for it is incredible that God is so powerful in terms of dead matter and helpless to deal with those human lives which he himself has brought into being as the crown of the natural process. It is surely not an accident which makes the psalmist put two sentences together: "He telleth the number of the stars. . . . He healeth the broken in heart."[1] Because he can do the first he can do the second. The wonder of the stars must not make him remote. The power that made the stars is the power at our disposal. Why, then, do we find it so hard to believe in it?

1. Because we rarely see it so impressively at work as we do in star, in waterfall, and wave. God doesn't seem, to us, to act in the realm of spirit as we think the Controller of stars and the Releaser of avalanches should act.

2. Because we have a mistaken idea of what power is in the realm of spirit, and therefore do not know where to look for its manifestations.

Frankly, the writers of the Old Testament are partly responsible for our difficulty. They also felt it and besought God to arise and let his enemies be scattered. "Why doesn't he *do* something?" they said. They were amazed that a Being with power in his hands, such as the stars and the waves revealed, should be so slow to lay bare his arm and act in human affairs as he acted in nature, with force which could be seen and applauded. *So they twisted natural events into divine judgments.* We have tended to do the same thing ever since.

For instance, when the tide overwhelmed the Egyptians in the Red Sea the devout Israelites saw the hand of God in it. We should open a subscription list for Egyptian wives and mothers if such a natural calamity happened today. We have done so repeatedly when natural calamities have swept thousands away. And I do not think the

[1] Psalm 147. 4 and 3.

dilemma can be avoided. God has not altered. If the Red-Sea incident were a divine judgment, why not call the Quetta earthquake by the same name? If you do not call the earthquake God's punishment, why do you give the Red-Sea calamity that significance? We cannot teach our children that God loves all nations alike now, but that he used to prefer Israelites to Egyptians so much that he turned the tides on the latter and drowned them. We must take all natural calamities together. God allows both earthquake and tidal wave, but he doesn't *send* either as instruments of wrath. I do not mean that God does not *use* such happenings. I am pleading that we land ourselves with an impossible conception of God if we allow that he plans to wipe out hundreds of his creatures by acts which fill his humblest and least spiritual worshipers with sympathy for the sufferers. God does not do on a huge scale what we would scorn to do even on a small scale, and should, indeed, be punished for doing by the most elementary ethical code in the world.

The Jews continually compensated for their inferiority complex in regard to fighting by a phantasy about God which had no relation to reality. The Jews were poor fighters. One invader after another wiped his feet on Palestine and passed on. So the Jews made a phantasy that God would descend out of heaven with the armies of the sky and save the chosen people. Did he? No! It is not his way. In 70 A.D. Titus put his armies round Jerusalem and all but brought Jewish history to a close.

Yet still, in 1935, people are expecting God, as they say, to intervene, to do something, that is, in the realm of human experience, equivalent, shall we say, to the launching of a new planet or the release of a thunderstorm.

something violent, dramatic, winning his way by ruthless methods of apparent "power."

Therefore, before we even try to understand how omnipotence is likely to operate, we ought to have some definition of what power is, and I submit this: that power is ability to achieve purpose. The power of a railway engine, or a motor car, or a gun, or a sermon, or an argument, or a God, can be included in such a definition. And the power of God, therefore, is ability to achieve the *purposes* of an infinitely wise, holy, loving Being—the power to achieve, finally, those purposes which his nature and character suggest, remembering that it is not a denial of his omnipotence to say that he cannot do anything which contradicts his own nature; anything which is intrinsically irrational or unworthy. I want the reader to hold in his mind the thought that nothing is an expression of God's power unless it expresses and helps to fulfill God's purpose.

Now, a great many people in practical life disbelieve in the power of God because they expect him, as they say, to *intervene*. "Why didn't he stop the World War?" they ask. "Why didn't he save my child?" "Why doesn't he vindicate the righteous?"

But to ask for intervention makes so many mistakes that we may tenderly say that it is infant-school thinking.

1. To intervene means to come in. To ask God therefore to intervene suggests that he is outside his universe and must be asked to come in suddenly and use his power. But he and all his energies are already operating within the universe, concerning which he is immanent as well as transcendent. He cannot "come in" because he is "in" already, as far as such words express his activity. All

his powers are already at work. When we say that God "acted," we mean that we have obeyed those conditions which govern the operation of his energies; but the energies were there all the time. God has not suddenly been persuaded to rouse himself and do something.

2. Intervention, further, as popularly understood, would mean self-confessed failure on the part of God. It would involve the confession that the universe, as he planned it and schemed it in the beginning, was inadequate; that there are contingencies and crises which he had not foreseen, and that therefore he had to rush in to save people from catastrophe because something had gone wrong, the possibility of which he had overlooked. His government is not one of ceaseless, capricious interference. It is one of rule according to moral law and infinite wisdom.

3. Intervention would mean, thirdly, chaos instead of cosmos; it would mean that we should never learn the laws of nature, for, at any moment, by the prayer or supplication of someone, their action would be altered. Such a universe would be more terrifying than the one some of us feel to be so hard. Let us grant that God may always "act" within his universe in a way surprising to us. Such an act we rightly believe in and call miracle. But when he acts thus, he does so by means of laws of which we are ignorant or of whose interaction with one another we are ignorant. Miracles do not show interference with the tendencies of law-abiding forces, but, rather, the goal which God desires they should normally reach. Miracles are the fulfilling of law, not its rupture. And since God has given us minds which work as ours do, we have the right to demand that the universe, so much of

which is unknown, shall at least be learnable. If fire should burn one day and freeze the next, if iron should expand one day under heat and contract the next, the universe would be a *uni*verse no longer, but a nightmare.

4. Intervention would mean that the members of his family at school, in that hard school we call Life, would never develop their own character by the method of trial and error; would not be resourceful, and, indeed, would soon cease to be human as we understand the word.

I think we must dismiss the idea of intervention in the popular sense of the word, seeing that such intervention is not an expression of power, for the simple reason that it would not achieve purpose.

I want to quote two illustrations which the late Miss Lily Dougall used in one of her books,[2] in order to show the unescapable dilemma which faced even omnipotence. A man had a wife who was not very strong, but who always imagined that she was far worse than she was and complained accordingly. The husband was a very strong man physically, and, at first, gave in to her. He used to carry her from room to room, or, if she wished it, out into the garden to the shade of an apple tree. Of course, as we should expect, the woman got worse and worse. She became a doll. He had to lift her and carry her everywhere. One day the husband, after taking the advice of competent persons, made up his mind that she was really quite able to walk out into the garden by herself, and he made her do it. He had to stand back and watch her stumble. In a sense he had the power to save her from falling; but it was his purpose, even to let her

[2] *God and the Struggle for Existence.* (Student Christian Movement Press. Ltd.) P. 110.

bruise herself, in order that she might learn to walk. It was therefore the exercise of a greater power to stand away. To intervene would have been weakness. To refrain was power. It was much harder to refrain. But it achieved his purpose, and we defined power as strength to achieve purpose. Again and again she complained. Again and again it would have been far easier to have carried her, but his new purpose demanded a greater expression of power, and he suffered something approaching anguish as he saw her fall. But, at last, she was cured, her character was strengthened, and happiness, which otherwise would have been impossible, was produced.

We may see the same point in another illustration: Two boys are playing on the nursery floor, one much older than the other. The elder is building a wonderful palace with bricks. The younger keeps knocking it down, not always knocking it down out of naughtiness but out of folly, not watching where he is putting his feet; or possibly out of ignorance, not knowing that there was a beautiful tower just behind where he stood. Four ways are open to the elder brother. 1. He can build all by himself and let the little one watch. And, to anticipate the meaning of our illustration, God adopted that method in the works of nature. He did not wait for us when he made the Himalayan snows, nor the instinct of a bee, nor the moonlight on the sea. He made part of his universe by himself. 2. The elder boy can strike the little one on the head every time he knocks it down. 3. He can intervene and catch his little brother's foot before he kicks it down or his hand before it strikes. But look at the fourth way—of co-operation. He can suffer the disappointment of seeing a thing wrecked, and yet, with tremendous patience, offering all the counsel and help which the little one is capable of receiving, he can help the little brother build it up again, so that he uses his brother's powers to their utmost in that co-operation.

Now, God is like the husband in the first illustration and the elder brother in the second. And *the human family, viewed as a unity,* is to be thought of as the wife in the first illustration and the little brother in the second. God stands back, though his heart grieves at our stumbling, our ignorance, our folly, our sin. It would be so easy, in one sense, for God to take a short cut and save us; but it would be weakness, for it would not achieve his purpose. He sees his castle of dreams come down in ruins. Your little one dies, your loved one is in agony, your friend loses all he has saved. There is misery and suffering and pain through ignorance and folly and sin while the Big Brother tries to teach us how to do better, helping all his little brothers together to build his world as he wants it to be. He has a purpose which continues to follow the individual. He has not done with the individual because he suffers through the family ignorance and folly and sin; but first let us see that God cannot use methods other than the ones that cost him, and us, most. For no other method achieves his purpose. Therefore no other method so fully expresses power. Many cannot see this point. "It doesn't look like power," they say. It doesn't. But that is because the conception of power is so distorted in our minds. Such people charge God, rather, with helplessness. They cannot see that to end his "helplessness" would be to create ours.

Now, I hope, we are getting warmer. We are beginning to glimpse his purpose. We defined power as ability to achieve his purpose. What is his purpose? We say very glibly, "To bring in the kingdom of God." But there again we keep on thinking of the kingdom of God as an outward happiness-for-all system; the establishment of a kind of world garden-suburb, advertisements of which we have seen on railway-station platforms. Everybody has his own detached house with hot and cold water in all the bedrooms. There is a beautiful picture of mother sitting in a basket chair in the shade of an apple tree, knitting—not mending, for in a perfect world nothing wears out. And father is pacing the lawn—a lawn which mows itself—smoking a beautiful cigar, and there are numbers of chubby-faced children playing ball in the foreground. No poverty, no sickness, no ugliness, no disorder. No cancer, no slums, no pain. In other words, we conceive the idea of the kingdom of God as an outward condition of happiness and prosperity.

Now, the first thing to remember about the kingdom of God is that it is an inward state of mind and heart. "The kingdom of God is within you." The purpose of God, therefore, is to produce that condition within the heart of man. We shall not get much further in understanding God's power until we have got that right into our ductless glands. The Kingdom only comes nearer as human hearts are changed and inner lives are brought into conformity with God's will.

The danger of conceiving the Kingdom as eternal happiness is that we make the greater mistake of thinking that external methods will bring it in; but as Professor H. H. Farmer, to whom I am indebted in this section, truly points out, it is inward. If God wins in hearts, he wins everywhere. If he fails there, he fails everywhere.

Instead of using the phrase, "the kingdom of God," let us put his purpose in other words. It is to get every member of his family to use, fully, his own resources, including—let us remember—the forces of faith and prayer, and to bring all into complete harmony with his will. And, therefore, nothing is effective as an instrument of power which is out of harmony with his will.

If this be true, how useless, from the point of view of God's kingdom, are many methods which are called methods of power! How can the mere use of force bring the kingdom of happy relationships? And the latter is a description of the only peace which will last. If force does *not* bring that relationship, how can force be viewed as power? It does not achieve purpose.

We speak of the power of the law, but the purpose of the law is to change the criminal into a good citizen. Merely to lock him up in jail does not usually do this. If it does not, it is not the power of the law at all. It is weakness, the weakness that abandons purpose.

Many of us have painful memories of what was thought of as power of the schoolmaster. But if the purpose of education is to make a good scholar of every lad, merely to put him out of the room or to flog him is more often a confession of abject weakness than an expression of power. The purpose is confessedly abandoned, at any rate for a time.

I am not here contending that all uses of force are unjustifiable. I am contending that much that is called power is not power at all, even in human relationships. What is called leadership is, at the moment I write, often impotence. How can you call a thing power which, when used, does not achieve real progress? How can you call a thing leadership which does not bring us where we want to be?

Hitler is said to be a great leader and to possess power. But his action in regard to the Jews, if accurately reported, is that old fear-causing method of persecuting those with whom you don't agree. His action is black treachery to the cause of progress in the world. His methods are not power. Truly seen, they are like so many other methods of falsely-called power. They are a confession that he cannot achieve his purposes without outraging personality. Unable to achieve purpose, he pushes away by violence the elements which he cannot manage. That is not power. It is crass weakness. That is not being a leader. It is being a bad-tempered, impotent child.

Look, by way of contrast, at God's way. It is to suffer, to love, to endure, to wait, to see hopes go down and desires temporarily frustrated, to take no short cuts, countenance no reprisals, attempt nothing by violence, and thus to achieve the divine purpose in a divine way, and change the hearts of men, even if it means an age-long bearing of a cross, the anguish of which we cannot fathom.

"What!" we say to God, "are you going to stand all that? What weakness!" But is it? "Why, if I were God," said a friend of mine, "I would at least have a brass plate on the door. Further, I would get a move on; I would lay about me. If I were on the throne, I would make some people's ears burn with boxing for their persistent neglect." And knowing my friend, I believe he would. When we turn to Saint Paul, we find that he does not share our common misconception of the power of God. He says clearly that nothing is an expression of the divine power which is not action toward the achievement of the divine purpose, and that the divine purpose is the changing of men's hearts, and that methods of violence, coercion, and force do not change men's hearts. So in the same sentence in which he talks about the cross he talks about the power of God. "We preach Christ crucified, unto Jews a stumbling block, and unto Gentiles foolishness; but unto them that are called, . . . Christ the power of God."[3] "Christ crucified . . . the power of God." I wonder if we shall ever get that so into our hearts that it will really influence our action and our thoughts? If Christ picks up a whip of small cords that would hardly hurt a baby and drives the oxen, not the men, out of the Temple, we say: "That is power. Now he is laying about him. That is how he ought to act." How many times was that incident quoted during the World War, as though to drive animals out of the Temple were a parallel with men blowing one another to bits! Paul points to a naked body of a deserted Christ hanging on a cross, and he says, "Christ the power of God." As one has said, "It is beyond all human recklessness of thought that God the Eternal Almightiness should be revealed in that pale body glimmering through the thick shadows of that awful night of pain and dereliction: that the true image of an omnipotent God should really be a defeated Man dying in the dark." But which has changed more lives, all the wars in the world between the "Powers"—significant word—all the newspaper articles, all the discussions, all the political speeches, all the resolutions of all the societies under the sun, or that one sublime deed when God himself, in Jesus, his Perfect Revealer, for love's sake, went to the cross?

[3] I Corinthians i. 23, 24.

So God, misunderstood through thousands of years, misunderstood by the chosen people, reveals himself in One who maintains, unbroken, an outgoing love to men, even though they do all they can do to sting him to retaliation. For see the power of the cross! Here is love indeed! You may take the physical expression of that love, you beat it, you lash it, you crown it with thorns, you nail it to a cross—and then? You cannot do anything more than kill the body in revolting circumstances. When you have crucified God, you cannot do anything else but sit down and watch him there. Probably you will break down and become changed. Few eyes could *see* the agony of God with any interior insight and remain unchanged. From the cross God *reigns* omnipotent, for love is the only omnipotence. And carry our heads as high as we may, they will bow before him at last. Believe as fiercely as we may that his methods are impracticable and that our methods of force, our stern, "practical" methods, are making the world sweet and clean, free and safe, and we shall realize at last that all such methods collapse and break down. We shall find that love that keeps on loving never breaks down. It may suffer all the signs of defeat, but it is never defeated. It haunts the mind and the conscience afterward and meets men in the quiet rooms of thought from which no violence and no locked doors can keep it; and because God has made us as we are, it can find subtly hidden in the depths of every man's nature that which would bring him to remorse and penitence. This is the way in which God wins. Thus he achieves his purposes. This is the secret of power, a power compared with which that revealed in the solar system is as nothing and that which fills the heavens with stars is as the power of a child rolling marbles along the nursery floor.

Let me close the chapter on a personal note. Before we finish talking about the power of God, should we not ask ourselves whether we, who are asking where it is manifested, are ourselves shutting it out? Can we, in some silence of the soul, even if we are suffering, let Christ put his finger on the place in our lives where our force is resisting his power, our sin, it may be, or our disbelief, or our false thinking as to what power is? For if only we would cease to resist him, he would fill us with power, and we should see a spiritual power which *could* be likened to the energies of nature. Once, at least, men felt such a spiritual power that they *did* compare it with the forces of nature. Pentecost was like a rushing mighty wind.

And can we also, in that silence, look into the face of Christ, who asks us not so much for our service as for ourselves? Our service is so often in the same category as false ideas of power. My laundry offers me service, the Bus Company offers me service, and I say to God, "I will serve you," and I equate that service with power. So many energetic extraverts have deserted God and entered his service instead, thinking "to advance his kingdom." Their lives are much weaker than if they offered God *themselves* to do what he liked with. Am I willing to look a perfect fool for his sake? Am I willing, if necessary, to be overlooked, to be scorned, to be misunderstood, to be lonely, to be humbled, to suffer, to put self out of the picture, to share the fellowship of his sufferings, even if it means to go to a cross? If we do that, we shall learn, at last, the meaning of his sorrow. We shall know the secret of his strength and peace. We shall see, even "in our darkest hour of trial and anguish, the shining of the eternal light."

With these thoughts in our mind we may admit that, in the sense in which the word is popularly misunderstood, God is not omnipotent except in an ultimate sense. But if we say that there are things God "cannot" do, it must always be with the mental reservation that this is because to do them—taking for granted they are reasonable—would be to conflict with his perfect wisdom and holiness; and this, as we have seen, is not a denial of omnipotence.

Yet we may go further. We may say that God, who is suffering in all human affliction, is doing everything that can be done, short of doing for man what he can learn to do for himself. God's Spirit is urging men, inspiring men, leading men on, longing, with a yearning that almost frightens one, that man should become all that he might be, and do all that he might do.

And I think we may take the final step in the argument, and say that finally, God, without interfering with man's free will for one moment, will win. Finally, without violation of the rights, sanctity, and dignity of human nature, I believe he will find a way.

More than that, I believe that not only will the final result be a complete victory for God, but the steps up to it, which now seem so often like defeat, will themselves be transformed into victories. This was God's way when Jesus was put to a cruel death by men. Not only did God bring to pass the resurrection as a triumph *over* death, but the cross also, which looked like defeat, which was the work of evil men, that too was transformed, and was itself a victory. He maketh "even the wrath of men to praise him," and at long last there will be nothing left on the debit side of the account. Every item will be a credit to God.

In the meantime we must be patient. The woman in our illustration must have been hungry for her husband's strength. Yet how hungry he must have been to take her in his arms when she stumbled! We cry out for God's strength, and power, and might, and wonder why he doesn't stop this war, this cancer, this suffering, this tyranny, this wrong. God, on his side, is eager to sweep out of the infinite and carry his own children beyond it all. But if he did so, the human race would cease to develop. His children could never make his dreams come true. Perhaps one who reads these words is suffering dreadfully in body or mind. My friend, a loving God bends over you, asking you to bear bravely your share of the burden of all the world, knowing that he shares it with you and can justify every pang of it at last.

If we are patient, and try to learn his meanings, the more shall we help him in his mighty purposes. And I believe that those purposes are so vast and glorious, beyond all guessing now, that, when they are achieved and consummated, all our sufferings and sorrows of today, even the agonies that nearly break our faith, the disasters that well-nigh overwhelm us, shall, seen from that fair country where God's age-long dreams come true, bulk as little as bulk now the pieces of a broken toy, strewn long years ago upon a nursery floor, over which, thinking then that all our little world was in ruins, we cried ourselves to sleep.

CHAPTER III

WHY DOES GOD ALLOW SUFFERING?

ANOTHER assumption, not indicated in the first chapter, is that God's method, in regard to the creation of the world, was a method more accurately described by the word "evolution" than by any term which suggests a sudden fiat from which the universe instantaneously sprang.

I am not committing myself to any particular theory of evolution, but suggesting that it is more reasonable to suppose that God made the world gradually, by long processes of gradual development, with possible emergences at certain points in the processes, than that he made all things suddenly by the word of his power, starting bright and early on Monday morning and finishing on Saturday afternoon about half-past four—in time for tea!

If we accept any view of evolution at all, we have probably long ago come to the conclusion that man is at present the crown of a long process of development, and that a great many of the mechanisms in his body and mind have come down to him from his animal ancestors.

Try to imagine one of our animal ancestors, in some primeval jungle, in a world in which God had never allowed pain to enter. The animal is lying, basking in the sunshine, enjoying life. But no pain of hunger ever warns it that it must eat to live. No pang of thirst ever hints that it must stretch its lazy limbs and go down to drink at the river. It requires little imagination to see how long it would live. But suppose a painless instinct could teach it to eat and drink. Let us then imagine that it catches its paw between two rocks, gashes it, and sprains a muscle. It feels no pain, we are imagining, and so it goes on walking on the injured foot until the flow of blood from the gash means that the animal dies from loss of blood.

Imagine another animal with a thorn in its breast. No feeling of pain warns it to endeavor to draw the thorn out with its teeth. It goes on until, possibly, irreparable harm is done. We probably need not spend much time in realizing that pain has been provided, primarily, as a safeguard to health. Pain flashes a warning to the brain that something is wrong, and if the necessary measures for healing and safety are within the capability of the animal then, they can be taken. It is difficult to avoid the conclusion that without pain our animal ancestors would have been exterminated before the evolutionary process became consummated in man.

Thanks to pain, a little child draws his hand away from the hot bars of the fire in time to save himself from having his hand destroyed or its subsequent usefulness irreparably damaged. And all who have to do with children are grateful for the pain which produces the child's quick response to take to some older and more capable person those little pains of the body with which he cannot deal.

Of course an objection must be anticipated at once. Many people see, in the pain of the animal world, not a beneficent providence but a cruelty which creates its own problem in their minds. In his novel, *The Undying Fire,* Mr. H. G. Wells paints a picture of a rabbit killed by a stoat, of the victims of a butcher bird spiked on the thorns of a hedge, of a bird in the mouth of a cat, and so on, until one might imagine that all God's creatures live in a meaningless hell of agony.

This is a question into which we must go with some care and at some length because it raises itself in the minds of all tender-hearted and thoughtful people.

The mistake we make is in supposing that the animal feels the same measure of pain that we should feel if we were subjected to a similar injury. Although, in one sense, an animal's reaction to pain may be as swift as ours, the *degree* of pain is nothing like so severe, for the simple reason that the mental centers in the animal's brain are not so highly developed. To lay a whip across the back of a horse, or stick a pin in a sleeping cat, discovers a reaction to pain as *swift* as that of a human being, but the *degree* is less and the shock is less, because the animal is at a lower stage of mental development, and his nervous system, though sensitive and quick to react, does not allow him to feel the pain to the same extent. The painfulness of pain depends not on the speed with which we react to it, but on the degree to which the mental centers are developed. One notices the fact that people belonging to races whose cultural development is far lower than ours do not suffer from a painful injury to the extent to which highly cultured, spiritually developed people suffer.

One of the penalties the race must pay for its own development is that with spiritual sensitiveness and aesthetic appreciation there must go, hand in hand, a greater poignancy in painful experiences. But, as one has put it, it is better to be a man in pain than a cabbage in ecstasy. For this very reason our Lord, who reached the summit of human sensitiveness, suffered as none other has done. Pain was far more awful to him than to his contemporaries. He could not bear his cross, though he was young and strong. Men often lingered two days on the cross. He died in a few hours—a fact which caused surprise. (Mark 15. 44.) "The mark of rank in nature is capacity for pain." No one else ever had the capacity to suffer as he did.

Relevant to the general argument is the interesting point that a surgeon, without the use of an anaesthetic, can perform an operation on a baby, which—again without an anaesthetic—would kill an adult. I have myself been present when a surgeon has operated without any anaesthetic on a young baby. The baby kicked violently. There is no doubt that he reacted to pain and was sensitive to it. But the degree of pain and the shock to the system could not be so great, because the mental centers which record the shock were not yet fully developed. They have not attained the complexity which they will attain in later life. The pain of the animal, therefore, is even much less in measure than that of a baby.

We must, of course, be kind to animals and spare them all possible pain. Nothing incenses one so much as cruelty to animals and birds. But it is obvious that if a boy tears the wings off a fly, the shock to the fly is not so great, in proportion, as if someone pulled the arms off the boy. I am afraid this may spoil the point of some admonitions to children to be kind to animals, admonitions beginning, "How would you like it if someone did that to you?" But truth compels one to point out that after the outrage—and it is such—the fly will still walk about. To pull the arms off a boy would probably kill him through shock apart from the purely physical injuries.

Further, we must notice another interesting point. The painfulness of pain depends largely on the condition of the mind. Many of us remember hearing men on the battlefield say that they never noticed the pain of a wound received until the excitement of the engagement was dying down. Livingstone is said to have reported that he did not feel the teeth of the lion in his shoulder on the memorable occasion when he was attacked, until after the excitement was over.

In the *British Medical Journal* Dr. Arthur J. Hall, Emeritus Professor of Medicine of Sheffield University, gave his opinion that patients suffering from certain mental disorders are not, as a rule, afflicted with pain when they develop physical diseases. Even painful illnesses like cancer and internal ulcerations seldom cause them much distress, and in cases of pneumonia he noticed a remarkable absence of the normal symptoms of pain, and of coughing and general distress. He said that the nervous systems of mentally disordered persons are deadened to pain because of the condition of the mind, as if the patient were under the influence of a mild anaesthetic.[1]

Experiments in hypnosis would tend to suggest the same conclusion, for under deep hypnosis I have myself demonstrated to a group of medical men and women that the touch of a finger or pencil can be made to feel like red-hot iron and can actually inflict a blister; while the touch of a hot iron also produces no pain at all, and the cut of a knife, sufficient to draw blood, is not felt.

When, therefore, we are thinking about pain in the

[1] *British Medical Journal*, January 26, 1934.

animal world and remember the hypnotic effect of the eyes of a snake upon a small bird, and possibly the similar effect a cat may have on a mouse, I think we are entitled to deduce that not only are the mental centers so undeveloped that the animal has not the capacity to feel what we should feel through a similar injury, but that, in many cases in which one animal preys on another, it is more than probable that there is a condition of mind similar to the condition of hypnosis, in which the painfulness of pain is reduced, or even entirely inhibited.

Remember, also, that in the animal world there is no looking forward or back. So Burns addresses the mouse which starts away with a panic in its breast because his plow disturbs its nest:

> "Still thou art blest, compared wi' me!
> The present only toucheth thee:
> But, och! I backward cast my e'e
> On prospects drear,
> An' forward tho' I cannot see
> I guess an' fear."

There is no prolonged preliminary terror, no capacity to feel for others, very little sickness and old age, and no bungling among the murderers of the jungle.

I realize that I cannot convince the reader on this most important point without quoting authorities. I therefore ask that the following statements be carefully considered:

The first is taken from Canon Streeter's book *Reality*.[2] "Nature is not the Garden of Eden we should like to find it; still less, however, is it the Hell that in some moods we picture. It is an imaginative fallacy to see, as one

[2] *Reality*, by B. H. Streeter, pp. 156ff. The Macmillan Company, New York.

awful totality, the pain of every living thing; pain is only felt by individuals, and in the animal world it would seem as if the individual's share is quite small. That capacity to feel on behalf of others, which adds so much to human sorrow, hardly there exists, so that the individual experiences little pain apart from the physical suffering which falls to its own lot. Again, we must not think of the animal world as if it consisted mainly of creatures like the horse and the dog, made exceptionally sensitive by centuries of selective breeding, soft nurture, and the education of human intercourse; nor even of these as if their capacity for feeling were in any way comparable to that of human beings. In the vast majority of living creatures, sensation, so far as we can judge, rarely reaches that level of acuteness which we should call definitely pain. The 'cloven worm' probably feels the cleaving process hardly more than I feel the paring of my nails; the squeal of a rabbit bitten by a stoat is not less loud, but probably indicates less actual pain than that of a small boy smacked by a firm but kind mama. Among animals disease is rare, and as a rule it either kills quickly or causes small discomfort. Death is swift, and, even if violent, is rarely very painful. The hawk's victim, until the moment of its death, has lived blithely unconscious and unapprehensive of its doom. Sudden fear either excites or calms; and there is some evidence that in the tiger's grip (even with a human being) fear inhibits feeling and produces anaesthesia in the prey. And if low capacity for sensation, while reducing pain, makes pleasure also much less keen, the impression one derives from watching wild life is that its dominant mood is a kind of suffused happiness. And where happiness ceases, death is usually at hand. Lastly, the animals can know little of the suffering (as of the pleasure) which inevitably accompanies man's enhanced capacity for memory and prevision. In their world disappointment, despair, bereavement, and remorse are, in anything like the sense in which we feel them, quite unknown. There is little sorrow, and there is no sin.

"But if our idea of the cruelty of nature is to a large extent a sympathetic fallacy, what of the waste? To take one out of a hundred possible examples: A herring spawns several hundred thousand eggs, of which on an average only about three will reach maturity. But they are *not* wasted; every one of them, whether as egg or tiny fish, becomes food for some other living creature. Is the hen's egg that I ate for breakfast wasted because it never reached the chicken stage? We may allow ourselves to wish that evolution had developed on entirely vegetarian lines; but so long as I enjoy mutton chop without a qualm, I cannot accuse nature because the lion feeds on an antelope, which in all probability lived more happily and died with perhaps less pain than the sheep from which I dine. . . .

"The consideration that, apart from man, the case for cruelty and waste in nature is not a strong one, is merely negative. Closer observation, however, points to a positive conclusion that there is operative in nature an active Will to Good. Kropotkin in his now classical treatise, *Mutual Aid,* shows that, at the level of consciousness attained in bird and animal life, friendly co-operation is the rule, hostility the exception—not only between members of the same species but even between different species. The one conspicuous exception, of course, is where carnivorous or insectivorous creatures prey upon smaller or weaker species. But, as already pointed out, the relation between the carnivorous species and their ordinary food is precisely the same as the relation that prevails between man and the chicken or the sheep. There is no more 'immorality,' and as little cruelty, in the one case as in the other."

Here is another authority. In his valuable book called *Providence,*[3] Dr. Griffith-Jones writes as follows: "There is no reason to believe that the animals spend their lives in a state of perpetual terror as some sentimentalists would fain have us believe; and if the successful kill has its joys, so has the successful flight. Nor is there any doubt that the fact of hunting and being hunted has high evolutionary value in developing beauty and swiftness of form, and in stimulating psychic development in countless ways. Safety and freedom from the need of making exertion are debilitating elements in the lot of all living beings, man included; it is the jeopardies and insecurities of life that have been the chief stimulants of both health and betterment in all the kingdoms of life and mind. Better a world in which living creatures have to hunt or escape by strenuous efforts than a placid existence where all is security and dullness, and no demand is made for the exercise of life's ultimate resources for survival and development. Such has been the creative method; and, stern though it be, there is benevolence at the heart of it."

I want to quote next a passage from Canon Raven's book called *The Creator Spirit,* in which he writes as follows:[4] "We have already protested against the mis-

[3] Vol. I, p. 155. Hodder & Stoughton.
[4] Vol. I, p. 155. Harvard University Press.

interpretation of animal behavior which explains the actions of protozoon and insect, of bird and beast by the analogy of human intelligence; a similar protest must be made against attributing our sensibilities to creatures differently organized. It is perhaps creditable to our sympathy that we should see in the writhings of the severed earth-worm or the landed trout the expression of an anguish of body and nerves like our own, that when Tommy robs a nest of its eggs we should ask him how he would like to have his baby sister thrown out of the nursery window. Cruelty in the children of men deserves the severest punishment: it is our business to treat all that lives with reverence and comradeship. But it is obvious that, even so, our attitude is curiously inconsistent. Every gardener prunes his roses and gathers his sweet peas; yet few can squash a caterpillar or smash a snail without a twinge of remorse. And if inconsistent, it is also unscientific. There is no reason at all to suppose that the million eggs of the cod which form the food of the herring feel any more of what we know as pain than the million grains of wheat which make our daily bread. On that point the evidence is conclusive. 'When a crab will calmly continue its meal upon a smaller crab while being itself leisurely devoured by a larger and stronger; when a lobster will voluntarily and spontaneously divest itself of its great claws if a heavy gun be fired over the water in which it is lying; when a dragonfly will devour fly after fly immediately after its abdomen has been torn from the rest of its body, and a wasp sip syrup while laboring—I will not say suffering—under a similar mutilation, it is quite clear that pain must practically be almost or altogether unknown.'[5] Pain is due in us to three chief factors, to the highly sensitive nervous system which accompanies the development of the higher areas of the brain, to the anticipation of hurt due to our foreknowledge of what is to come, and to the sympathy which enables us to share the sufferings of our fellows. It has its physical, its psychic, and its spiritual sides, corresponding in its intensity to the level of our personality. A nerve-net, a faculty of bare cognition, a mere 'relateness' with other organisms—creatures so equipped do not and cannot share our sorrows. As they rise in the scale of life, as new powers emerge in them, there is development of sensibility; but the difference is so vast between the primitive and the civilized races of mankind that it may be doubted whether there is any real pain without a frontal cortex, a fore-plan in mind, and a love which can put itself in the place of another; and these are attributes of humanity. The others suffer, each in the measure of its capacity; their range is not ours, nor anything at all closely resembling it. And to assume it to be so is to set up the bogey of a nightmare as truth."

Darwin made much of the way in which parasites lived within the body of the caterpillar, but it has been shown since that the caterpillar knows nothing about it. There are millions of things living on us at the present moment, however clean we may be in our habits, but we know nothing about it.

Dr. Alfred Russell Wallace probably knew as much as anybody about our present subject, and his conclusion is certainly worth quoting. He says: "The piteous picture

[5] The Rev. Theodore Wood, quoted by Simpson, *The Spiritual Interpretation of Nature*, pp. 131-2.

of nature, 'red in tooth and claw with ravine,' is a picture the evil of which is read into it by our imaginations, the reality being made up of full and happy lives usually terminated by the quickest and least painful of deaths. . . . The supposed torments and miseries of animals have little real existence, but are the reflection of the imagined sensations of cultivated men and women in similar circumstances; and the amount of actual suffering caused by the struggle among animals is altogether insignificant."[6] And Sir E. Ray Lankester supports such a conclusion. In one of the Romanes Lectures he says: "It is a remarkable thing that the adjustment of organisms to their surroundings is so severely complete in nature, apart from man, that diseases are unknown as constant and normal phenomena under those conditions. Every disease to which animals (and probably plants) are liable, except as a transient and very exceptional occurrence, is due to man's interference."[7]

I think we have enough evidence there for our conclusion in regard to the pain of animals. Its purpose is wholly beneficent and its existence, *apart from the interference of man,* cannot be thought of as evil. Whether we are justified in *causing* pain to animals in order to benefit man is a big question, and we cannot do justice to it here. All of us who love animals and who have had—as I have had—the rich gift of the friendship of a dog, a cat, or a horse, find it hard not to protest passionately against some experiments of which we read. Yet when I think of the thousands of human beings definitely benefited because animals have been sacrificed, I find that I

---

[6] *Darwinism,* p. 40; compare also the same author's *The World of Life,* pp. 380 ff.
[7] *Romanes Lecture* for 1905, pp. 28ff.

come down on the side of the vivisectionists. But they must show us that their experiments bring real benefit, that every one of them is absolutely necessary and that precautions are taken to exclude every pang of unnecessary pain from our dumb friends who give their lives for us. It is a true response in personality which rouses us to righteous anger if animals suffer unnecessarily and which makes us punish severely those who are cruel to them. I confess I love Ralph Hodgson's poem:

> "'Twould ring the bells of heaven,
>   The wildest peal for years,
> If parson lost his senses
>   And people came to theirs,
> And he and they together
>   Knelt down with angry prayers
> For tamed and shabby tigers,
>   And dancing dogs and bears,
> And wretched, blind pit-ponies,
>   And little hunted hares."[8]

And F. L. Ghey's prayer wins a deep response from most of us:

> "Hear our humble prayer, O God, for our friends the animals. In thy hand is the soul of every living thing, and we bless thee that thou carest for the dumb creatures of the earth. We bless and praise thee for thy joy in their beauty and grace, and we desire to share thy love for them all.
>
> "Accept our prayer especially for animals who are suffering: for all that are overworked and underfed and cruelly treated: for all wistful creatures in captivity,

---

[8] Quoted by special permission of the author and the publishers, The Macmillan Company.

that beat against their bars: for any that are hunted or lost or deserted or frightened or hungry: for all that are in pain or dying: for all that must be put to death. We entreat for them all thy mercy and pity, and for those who deal with them we ask a heart of compassion, and gentle hands, and kindly words. Make us ourselves to be true friends to animals and so to share the blessing of the merciful.

"For the sake of thy Son the tender-hearted, Jesus Christ our Lord. Amen."

We must turn back to the pain of man.

Imagine a primitive man lifting a burning log and feeling no pain. Then the hand of the man, his most perfect tool, is destroyed and useless. So man brings from his animal ancestry ability to feel pain, pain which is a safeguard to health and a teacher of nature's laws, and he cannot altogether complain if the development of his mental centers—such an amazing asset to him in the developed life which he has come to live—carries with it liability as well as asset and means a greater capacity to suffer. A highly developed mental and nervous equipment means the possibility of a far greater degree of pleasure; but this is inseparable from the possibility of a far greater degree of pain.

Sherrington calls pain "the psychical adjunct of an imperative protective reflex."[9] Then he goes on to say that scattered over our skin in countless numbers are pain-points which he calls noci-ceptors, fibrils of nerve tissue, bared of their sheaths like pieces of electric wire stripped of their insulating coverings. They end among

[9] *Affirmations*, Dr. R. W MacKenna, M.A., M.D. Ernest Benn, Ltd.

the cells of the skin. They are especially designed to watch for, to pick up, and to transmit to the brain, immediate information about any hurtful attack made upon the skin. If these are asleep or out of action, as sometimes happens in disease, serious damage may be done to the body before the mind is aware of it. Hence we pull away our fingers at once if something is too hot to be comfortable. Some parts of the body have more pain-points than others, such as the fingers, and the soles of the feet. The brain, thought to be so very sensitive, has none, for it is guarded not only by the bony skull, but, beneath that, by muscle and membrane. It is safe from any injury from the outside except of the most violent kind, and has therefore no need for the pain-points which other parts of the body must have as defensive mechanisms. It is said that the brain, if it could be laid open without the pain of injury to its protective coverings, could be cut or burnt or probed in a conscious patient and that he would feel no pain.

Dr. R. W. MacKenna, in his excellent booklet already quoted, works out in the most able manner the point that a man's safety depends on his capacity for feeling pain. He shows that there is no pain too paltry for notice. That there are no real "growing pains." For instance, he thinks that many a child has struggled through life with a damaged heart because nature's signal of pain, proclaiming the presence of a rheumatic infection, was treated casually by some stupid parent who shut his ears to the message and put the little sufferer off with the words, "It is only a growing pain." He gives a most diverting explanation of the pain of a boil and that of an appendix, which I have permission to quote. "Boils are due to a local infection with a pus-producing microorganism. In a flaccid, toneless condition of the muscles round the site of the boil, the suppuration, instead of remaining definitely local, might spread widely. Therefore there is always a protective muscular reflex; the sufferer has a 'stiff-neck'—and with it there is the accompanying symptom of pain.

"The fine adjustment of pain to the best service of the sufferer is singularly manifested in that common disease appendicitis. In the early stages there is pain, at first diffuse over the abdomen, but soon concentrated immediately over the appendix. And with the pain there is its accompanying protective reflex of muscular rigidity. The muscles over the appendix become tense and hard. This fulfills two purposes. It lessens the sufferer's pain, because the abdominal wall no longer moves freely in the act of breathing, and, further, it protects the appendix from external pressure, and coincidently insures that condition of immobilization which is a useful adjunct to the processes of defense and repair. But sometimes, in appendicitis, there is a sudden abatement or disappearance of pain, although the other symptoms of raised temperature and quickened pulse may still be alarming. The friends of the patient may be lulled into a state of false security by the abatement of the pain; but the surgeon, from experience, knows the new danger that has arisen. The appendix has died—perished in the fires of inflammation—or it may have ruptured. Pain is no longer of use in defense. Already the chemical laboratories in the body are working at high pressure, for now, short of surgical aid, the patient's safety depends on their efficiency; and as pain would hinder now, rather than help, it has ceased to proclaim itself."

I have frequently met doctors who wish that pain were more insistent in calling attention to what is wrong. I recall that a medical student is instructed never to give morphia until the doctor or specialist has made his diagnosis; and a Leeds specialist once told me that after a very severe illness due to microbic invasion (say pneumonia), the heart is poisoned. There is no pain in the heart—that is the misfortune. "A patient," he said, "apparently quite well, may get out of bed and die instantly. He has not been warned by pain to wait until his heart has fully recovered." All of us have suffered the punches of doctors who go on punching till they find where it hurts most. Then they seem happy. We may note here that the pain of a sprain not only warns us that something is wrong with part of our machinery, but it stops that part of the machine from working until repairs have been carried out. Pain is both signal and protection, not allowing the injured member to be used until the injury is repaired. Without pain all death would be sudden. Thanks to the signal, many injuries about which we should otherwise know nothing can be repaired and death warded off.

When we come to the pain suffered by those who contract diseases caused by germs, we are met with a real problem as to why germs were created at all. Some would say at once that they were created by the devil; but this would mean a dualism in nature which makes, I think, more problems than it solves. At the same time we must not dismiss as fantastic the supposition that the whole of the universe is definitely out of gear. Doctor Maltby once said that the universe was like a gorgeous house and grounds, all in disorder because its tenant was drunk, the tenant, in this case, being man. And the question is worth trying to think out. Since God has made a universe with men in it who have free will, who learn slowly, who are blind, ignorant, and foolish; since the universe contains free spirits who have been in rebellion against God; since there are vibrations in the universe which are out of harmony with his intention, may those vibrations not have invaded the whole scheme of things? The universe is a *uni*verse. It is a complex but unified whole. Who can suppose that if once an inharmonious element is allowed in it, such as the misused free will of man, the harm done can be localized? If a painful boil only an inch or two in size can throw my whole body and brain out of gear so that I feel too ill to do my work, what is the result on the body of nature of so vast a thing as the sin of man with its many implications? May it not be that many things have come to exist in the universe which God never intended to be? Such a conception is not far from biblical teaching. The author of the parable in Genesis tells us thorns and thistles grew in the Garden because man had sinned.[10] And Saint Paul certainly talks about the whole creation groaning and travailing in pain waiting for man's redemption.[11] We may not see the link between a disharmony in nature and a disharmony in man's relation to God; but we are so closely bound to the universe that disharmony at one point in it may easily involve disharmony at another.

It may be true that germs would never have come into being, that is, germs of disease, but for man's sin and folly. It is certainly not a complete parallel, but the way

---

[10] Genesis 3. 18.
[11] Romans 8. 22, 23.

in which we have dealt with the mosquito, and the way in which certain parts of the tropics are now completely free, make it possible for one to say that the presence of the malaria mosquito indicates ignorance or slackness on the part of man. At least there are methods of action open to man which leave the malaria mosquito no place to breed or propagate.

Another suggestion has been made: that the presence of a germ, and the disease set up by a germ, constitute another form of warning of something wrong in the system, so that reaction can speedily be met to save the whole organism from death.

For myself I find help in the view that what we call the germ of disease may be a good thing, with functions not wholly understood, but valuable in the scheme of things except when the functioning takes place in the human body. I remember only too vividly how we hated the sandflies which bit us during the Mesopotamian campaign and gave us so-called sandfly fever. Having suffered myself from this particular nuisance when a young staff officer under the Political Department, compelled to ride for miles on horseback from one Arab sheikh to another, and to sleep on the open desert far from the devices available in civilization, I speak feelingly. We made up a ribald song which ran as follows:

> "I wouldn't choose
> To live with the Jews,
> Or the Arab tribes we see.
> Farewell little hell,
> Sandfly goodbye,
> There's a blighty girl waiting for me."

It was a real problem to understand what good exactly the creation of the sandfly had done. As a Tommy said to me in a camp far up the Euphrates, "Why did God waste time making the b——— things?" But a conversation with an Arab sheikh put the matter in a different light. "We cannot get on without sandflies," he said, "because they fertilize the date palms. Without the sandfly we should have no dates and without the dates we could not live." Further, the Arab himself has developed an immunity from the sandfly and seems never to be troubled by it.

For many years I regarded the wasp as an unmitigated nuisance. One might ask impatiently why God made wasps. But an expert corrected the objection of ignorance. He wrote as follows: "Nine tenths or more of the activities of wasps are beneficent. From late spring to early autumn they seek out and destroy vast multitudes of caterpillars and grubs, which, if left unchecked, would destroy our crops, our vegetables, our orchards, and our trees." I cannot tell why God created those germs which to us spell disease, but I have no right to make a petulant outcry based merely on ignorance of the possible beneficent *raison dêtre* of all that God's hands have planned.

I do not know why God made the germ of diphtheria. I can only guess that the diphtheria germ has fulfilled a useful function, and may even now play a scavenger's part. At the same time it is part of the battle to which humanity is committed to banish diphtheria *from the places where men live* and to produce an immunity from the attacks of similar bacilli. I cannot tell you why God made a tiger or a bear. I presume there is a purpose could we but understand it; but just as our ancestors waged unceasing battle against wild beasts of great size and ferocity, so we now have the same battle to fight, only the wild beasts we have to tackle can only be seen through the microscope. But the struggle is the same and the problem is no different. We have banished cholera and plague. We must use our resources similarly to banish other diseases.

If I were a dictator I would take all the specialists who are doing much magnificent work in research concerning the cause, prevention, and treatment of disease: I would put all the financial resources they needed at their disposal and give them every facility for getting on with their glorious task. It is irrational for man plaintively to ask why God should allow him to become smitten by disease when the money spent on a couple of battleships would enable researchers quite shortly to wipe out the scourges which afflict us without much more difficulty than that faced by many an Indian villager who, with or without outside help, has rid his village of man-eating tigers. It will be time to present the problem of germ-infection and illness generally, as part of the mystery of pain and a kind of indictment of the goodness of God, when, if ever, it can be proved that the resources open to man must finally fail to deal adequately with the situation.

CHAPTER IV

WHY DO THE INNOCENT SUFFER?

The problem of suffering would be far less poignant if we could show that suffering always followed the conscious and deliberate breaking of some rule. What makes the problem so torturing to many minds is that people suffer for causes which are not their fault at all; even little children endure anguish in a way that wrings our heart, until we are tempted to lose faith in God, since some of his actions seem to be comparable with that of one who, not content that his children shall suffer for their own misdeeds, allows a trap to be set for them in the dark, so that they suffer agonies without any possibility of avoiding the pain or understanding why they suffer so.

One hardly supposes that a question which has been an outstanding problem since the time the book of Job was written can be answered within the compass of one small chapter, yet possibly, even within those limits, one can indicate certain lines of thought along which an answer may be felt if not completely seen.

Let us ask what possibilities lay open to God when he made those plans which human life should follow. One of the very wisest and most beneficent of these plans we may call the plan of the great human family. I mean by this that God chose—because it was the best method of all those open to him—to arrange human life on the basis of the family. We are members one of another. We literally cannot live entirely to ourselves. We depend on one another.

We can see how wise this is if we imagine life arranged on the basis of the individual instead of the family. Had God chosen the former method, then nothing would have come to us through the misdeeds or ignorance or folly of others, but, also, nothing would have come to us through the wisdom, courage, and nobility of others. We should not have to carry the burden of others. But neither should we ever be carried by the wings of others. Nothing undeserved, whether an asset or a liability, would ever have come to us. We should live an individual life. The innocent would never suffer.

To conceive of an existence where everything was cut off from us that did not come to us through our own merit, is to feel a tremendous relief that the government of the world is in the hands of a God who saw far enough ahead to plan the world on the family basis and save us from the curse of individualism. Take one example. Suppose you fell ill through your own fault. No wisdom could be at your disposal save your own; no kindly sympathy or nursing; no invention of other men's brains; no skill of other men's fingers. What happens today? You are whirled to hospital in a car which, in itself, represents the brains of a thousand men through a long period of years. At the hospital you are tended by the patient skill and nursing of others. Inventions of brilliant men of all nations and all ages are at your disposal through the training the doctor has had. In a word, the brains and the skill of the family are at your beck and call. As an individualist you would have died like a dog in a ditch.

Nor is it only in emergency that we gain from belonging to the family. When I rise and go to my bath, a cake of soap is handed me by a Frenchman, a sponge is handed me by a Pacific Islander, a towel by a Turk, my underclothes by one American or Englishman, my outer garments by another. I come down to breakfast. My tea is poured out by an Indian or a Chinese. My porridge is served by a Scottish farmer. My toast I accept at the hands of an English-speaking farmer, not to mention the baker. My marmalade is passed to me by a Spaniard, my banana by a West Indian. I am indebted to half the world before I have finished breakfast. The secret of half my happiness is that I belong to a family. As Newman pointed out in his great sermon on "The World's Benefactors," we are indebted to hosts of men and women forever unknown. He says, "Those men are not necessarily the most useful men in their generation, nor the most favored of God, who make the most noise in the world and who seem to be principals in the great changes and events recorded in history. . . ." We do not know "who was the first cultivator of corn; who first tamed and domesticated the animals whose strength we use and which we make our food; who first discovered the medicinal herbs which, from the earliest times, have been our resource against disease." Why, if ever the choice had been given to us and we had been wise, we should have chosen life on the family basis rather than life on the basis of the individual.

To imagine life on the individual basis leads us to a situation which is amusing to contemplate, but would be no fun to realize. No clothes would be available save those we could make for ourselves, presumably from the skins of beasts; since, if we are not to have the fruits of other men's labors, nothing woven for us is available.

We should sally out to try to procure breakfast with no weapon save that which we ourselves could fashion.

As I sit at my desk I realize that any good I can do through writing these words is a good only possible through the co-operation, literally, of hundreds of my brothers. I think of the pen with which I write, the electric light, the warmth of the fire, the friendly books on the shelves which line the room, the subsequent co-operation of publishers, printers, proofreaders, retailers, and travelers and a score of other helpers, without whom the sending out of this message would be impossible.

Shall we, then, receiving such untold benefit from our membership of the family, deem it unfair when we are asked to bear the consequences of the family ignorance, the family folly, the family sin? Shall I cry to God and say, "Why did you make a world like this?" when I have just decided that this is the best choice that lay before God himself, that my best judgment confirms his choice and that, as we saw on p. 26, even omnipotence does not make possible the use of both choices when they are mutually exclusive? God cannot give me the benefits of the family life without its risks and liabilities. I cannot have all I want from both the family basis of life and the individual basis of life and the woes of neither. Each choice excludes the other. Let me admit how terrible the liabilities are. Never a week passes but I hear or meet instances of what folk suffer because of other people's mistakes or sins. As I write these words news comes of a distinguished doctor at work in the ward of a hospital. A nurse, near by, is cleaning a hypodermic syringe, pointing it upward. She holds it by the barrel, forgetting to hold the needle also. As she energetically works the piston, the needle flies off and passes into the doctor's eye. It is the eye he uses for his specialized work with a microscope. The sight is irrevocably lost.

Before me lies the letter of a broken-hearted widow who had an only child, a daughter of thirteen. The child had her tonsils removed, and was discharged from the hospital on a day of thick fog. She caught a chill, developed pneumonia and died. Her mother is inconsolable. "Eileen was all I had left," she cries.

I could fill this book with the heartbreaking incidents I have personally met with in my work; and though I protested when a nurse said to me, "No one who has nursed cancer patients can believe in God," I know how she felt.

To enter a family is not only to take over the family assets, but the liabilities; not only the family joys, but the family sorrows. I need not rack my soul with the torturing thought that my illness and pain are my fault. I may be suffering for the family. I may be one of those of whom Carlyle wrote, "For us was thy back bent, for us were thy straight limbs and fingers so deformed; thou wert our conscript on whom the lot fell, and fighting our battles wast so marred." If a local football team makes a mistake in tactics and in the effort to redeem the mistake one of the players is hurt, does he cry out against it as unjust? Does he ask why the innocent should suffer? No, he accepts it as part of the game. He is helping the team to win through. These may seem hard words to some lonely sufferer; and in truth there is a greater word for him, as we shall see; but there is light for many in the thought that God was faced with a real alternative in making the basis of life that of the family or the unit, that the latter choice would have brought far more pain to the individual, and that selfishness would have been a greater evil than suffering. There would never be any happiness for a worthy individual in a private escape from suffering to which others were exposed. Solitary comforts are poor things. The very essence of our best self is love, and love wants to share not only pleasures but pain. Love would refuse an emancipation from pain which only included the self, just as love rejects the thought of salvation which is not available for every son of man. The thought which, for the noblest men and women on earth, would make life intolerable if carried into effect, is that they should be excluded totally from the pain of others.

Omar Khayyám in one of his stanzas says he would like

> "To grasp this sorry Scheme of Things entire,
> . . . Shatter it to bits—and then
> Remold it nearer to the Heart's desire!"

But is there any way known to man by which it could be remolded nearer to the desire of the *greatest hearts?* The question gives me the chance to quote some great words of Dr. James Martineau. Preaching on "The Uncertainties of Life" he says: "A world without a contingency or an agony could have no hero and no saint, and enable no son of man to discover that he was a son of God. But for the suspended plot that is folded in every life, history is a dead chronicle of what was known before as well as after; art sinks to the photograph of a moment, that hints at nothing else; and poetry breaks the chords and throws the lyre away. There is no Epic of the Certainties and no lyric without the surprise of sorrow and the sigh of fear. Whatever touches and ennobles us in the lives and in the voices of the past is a divine birth from human doubt and pain. Let then the shadows lie, and the perspective of the light still deepen beyond our view; else, while we work together, our hearts will never burn within us as we go, and the darkness, as it falls, will deliver us into no Hand that is divine."

Granted, then, that the family basis is the best basis, we must learn the responsibilities of belonging to the family. The very laws which make it possible for us, by a clean, healthy, pure life, to pass on that most glorious of all bequests, a sound stamina to our children, make it also possible for us to pass on venereal disease. The glory of being a member of a family carries with it its obligation. If you live on a desert island, you can lose your temper, be irritable, behave like a pig, and it won"t affect anyone else. But in a family you will make others miserable. We must continually pull ourselves up not only with the question why the innocent suffer, but whether we are behaving in a way which may cause future innocents to suffer.

So I think we must accept the basis of the family as the best of all possible bases. We must see that from the family we gain far more than we lose. We must beware lest, by our own folly or sin, we leave a legacy of pain to those who follow after. We must take up the family burden, happy to know that God himself honors it. He honors it by ordaining that he himself shall be mediated to men through it. I mean this, that though he has ways of touching our lives directly, yet again and again by his own self-limitation he waits and withholds what he himself desires for us, until some other member of the great human family comes to our aid with loving heart or clever brain or skillful fingers. Whatever may lie ahead of us, at present, at any rate, God's own purposes are held up until the family wakes up to its resources and its responsibilities.

One lovely morning some months ago I was walking with a friend in a wood near X, where I had been privileged to see some of the excellent work he is doing in that town. Our conversation turned to the problem of providing for our old age or in case of premature death. From this gloomy consideration our thoughts naturally turned to Jesus' teaching about the lilies and birds.

"Behold the birds of the heaven, that they sow not, neither do they reap, nor gather into barns; and your heavenly Father feedeth them. Are not ye of much more value than they? . . . If God doth so clothe the grass of the field . . . shall he not much more clothe you? . . . Be not therefore anxious." I suppose these words in Saint Matthew's Gospel enshrine one of the loveliest idyls in the New Testament. It produces a vaguely pleasing impression like Tennyson's poetry; but is it reliable? Is it an idyl, or is it an argument? Is it a picture to please the aesthetic senses, or is it a rock on which the soul can build?

Later in the day my friend showed me some of the slums of X, and my mind was busy with Jesus' picture. Here is a man with six children and an ailing wife, living in a filthy hovel for which they pay a high rent. The man's spirit is broken; there is no food, no coal, insufficient clothing. Unfortunately, this is not an overdrawn picture. It is not easy to look up to God at all when you have an empty stomach, a pile of bills, a sick wife, and children that cry night after night from hunger. Supposing I had gone into his cottage, pulled out a Testament and read: "Be not anxious what ye shall eat or what ye shall drink, nor yet for your body what ye shall put on. Behold the birds of the heaven. Your heavenly Father feedeth them; are not ye of much more value than they? Consider the lilies . . . if God so clothe the grass of the field shall he not much more clothe you?" Would it not be a cruel farce to read such words in such a place? What did Jesus mean?

Let us try to think the matter out. God has provided enough for all his creatures. If you think of the things we eat and wear, you will find that they go back in their origins to something God has provided. Moreover, he has provided enough. World figures have shown year after year that famine in Russia or failure in India has been balanced by bumper crops in Canada. Given the good will of the community, in these days of easy transport, there is no reason on God's side why every man and woman should not have enough to eat and enough to wear.

But God depends on men to act as brothers in order that his providence may be mediated. He has set us in a great human family because life on an individual basis—which is the alternative—would be impossible as well as unethical. But this family basis of life means that he can be temporarily defeated by the selfishness of man.

All this is true, but would it be any message to the dweller in the slums if on that sunny day we had explained to him thus, "Of course God has provided enough. God means you to have enough, but owing to the selfishness of man you cannot have your share and God is thus defeated"? He might reasonably say, "It is good of you to explain, but that does not fill my stomach, pay my rent, or even satisfy my mind."

I think it is better to say at once that Jesus' message about birds and lilies is not an idyl but an argument. But it is an argument about the nature of God—not how he will act by imagined omnipotence in this or that case, but what his nature is. And it is that he loves and cares. For reasons we have seen he cannot, or does not, interfere when his will is thwarted; but the great anchorage of the soul is that he goes on loving and caring, and that all happenings are in his hands so that, though we cannot explain or even thwart disaster, we can bear it. As Doctor Maltby says: "Jesus did not show us how to explain the tragedies of earth. He showed us how to bear the thought of them."

Moreover, Jesus, who quoted the birds as illustrating God's providence, was far too keen a student of nature not to notice the sparrow's fall. It did not escape him that God does not intervene if birds quarrel—if they, like men, are selfish, if they snatch things from one another, if the cuckoo pushes wee fluffy things out of the nest, if the hawk sweeps down with seeming cruel beak and talon, if the cat catches the bird in sharp claws, if boys stone a chaffinch and break its wings, if some rough hand takes the skylark and pushes it within a tiny cage. God does not interfere, and the question why he does not would take us too far from our purpose here. But the anchor of the soul is Jesus' word that God loves and cares and is concerned, and is with the sparrow when it falls.

I think that thought of his that "not a sparrow falleth to the ground without your heavenly Father," is one of the tenderest in the New Testament. So moving is it that when, a few weeks ago, I saw a dead sparrow on the grass of the great court at Trinity College, Cambridge, I had a queer impulse to take it up and bury it tenderly for the sake of the One who was with it when it fell.

The main point of the argument about birds and lilies, then, is Jesus' attempt to prove the nature of God. Could we paraphrase like this?

"Don't worry overmuch about clothes and food. Your Heavenly Father knows you have need of these things, and because he has given them to the birds and lilies you may be sure he is anxious for you to have them and has made provision for his human family. And although men defeat his will, he is very eager that his Spirit shall so spread that all men will be supplied. When his kingdom is here and his justice is done, men will share, and find enough for all. Seek, then, his kingdom and his righteousness and all life's necessities will be yours. At the same time do not be obsessed by those things. That is what the heathen do. Remember that there are greater things in life than either food or clothes. Lay up treasure in heaven; realize your relation with God—a God of love who can bring to you now something greater than food, something greater than shelter."

Jesus is not asserting that God guards birds and lilies from harm, for the former die and the latter are cast into the oven. He is asserting that God is concerned with them, and when I see the birds and the lilies I am not to misconstrue Jesus' argument so as to suppose that I shall inevitably be provided for, but I am to regard birds and lilies as symbols of the concern of God in a world that is hard and often cruel. Beauty is like a glance of love from a friend in the midst of a hostile crowd; a hand pressure, a caress, to those weighed down with the traffic of the market place; a word of appreciation to a man discouraged."[1] In a world in which other things shriek at us that life is hard, merciless, arrogant, selfish, the birds and lilies show that the heart of the universe is friendly. God is love and God cares about you. "If I show you a rose," said Tertullian, "you will not find fault with God any more." For, of course, it is absurd to suppose that the life-process, which makes a lily or a skylark, is not seeking to work through man in love and care. If the heart of the universe were not friendly, were cruel, were merciless, lilies and birds would be impossible.

At the same time let me make one last point very clear. God expects his children to mediate his providence to one another. It is not his will that one child in his family should have so much of this world's goods that he hardly knows what to do with it, and that another child in his family, willing to serve the community, should not have enough to feed or clothe his little ones. God help us at the last if by hoarding unnecessary wealth we are depriving another needy child of God of his birthright! This is the point of the comparison with Solomon. The amassing of treasure for oneself, in spite of a consciousness of the need of others, is hostility to God, whose gifts were meant for all his children.

We often wish that God would destroy slums, prevent immorality, hinder evil, cure bodies and minds. *But the*

---

[1] Professor H. H. Farmer. *Things Unseen*, p. 53. James Nisbet & Co., Ltd.

awakened responsibility of the family is what God is waiting for. This family basis we have been considering involves a terrible responsibility not only to man who suffers when it is not responded to, but to God himself, for it puts a restraint on God's purposes. "Why do I need psychoanalysis?" said a patient to me. "Can't God heal me?" One might as well say, on developing acute appendicitis: "Why do I need a surgeon? Can't God help me?" The point is not what God can do, but what he does do. And the fact is that he presses us to live as a family and recognize the family fact by making us depend on one another. God has even entered this wondrous family and bears, in a sense, that which our limitations prevent us from realizing, all its pain and sorrow on his own heart. He himself, unutterably pure, the Holy and Innocent One, silences our fretful question, "Why do the innocent suffer?" by revealing his own anguish. God cannot prevent the possibility of the suffering of the innocent without rearranging life on a basis which even we see to be less good.

Dr. Chrichton-Miller, in his book *The New Psychology and the Preacher,*[2] gives an illustration which I have permission to reproduce here: As an important express was about to leave a London terminus, an agitated lady assailed the stationmaster and begged him to postpone the departure of the train.

He told her he had no power to do so, and that the only man who could was the general manager. She rushed to his office and repeated her request. "We have just heard," she said, "that our boy has met with a serious accident and is not expected to live. My husband is on

[2] P. 209. Published by Jarrolds, London.

his way, but he cannot possibly arrive until fifteen minutes after the hour of departure. If you keep the train waiting, you will be giving him the only chance of seeing the boy alive. Surely, if you have any spark of human sympathy you will not refuse!" The general manager said: "Madam, I am very sorry for you and for your husband, but I cannot do it."

"You mean you won't do it," she said. "You made the timetable of this railway, so, of course, you could hold the train up if you wished to."

"Madam," he said, "the train makes more than one important connection which would be lost if I delayed it. There may be others in the train to whom the catching of one of these connections may mean just as much as to your husband. My business is to serve the community by maintaining the most trustworthy railway service that is possible."

There is a further word for the individual, a message which I think covers his individual problem; but our illustration does show us the only possible basis on which a train service can be run, and more importantly, the only possible basis on which a universe can be run.

It is a commonplace to say that if two consequences follow from a given proposition, we cannot plaintively ask to have the one without the other, even though one may strike us as pleasing and beneficial and the other seem evil and hurtful. Our statement of omnipotence in the first chapter does not define power as the capacity to produce what is inherently impossible. The laws of logic express the Divine Mind as they hold sway in our own, and if we allow that the original basis of the universe is the best, we cannot, by any juggling, exclude such painful consequences as are bound to flow from it, though some of them are admittedly very deeply distressing.

Here I wish to quote some wise words of Dr. F. R. Tennant:[3] "That there could be a determinate evolutionary world from which all such events were excluded, a world of unalloyed happiness and comfort and yet a law-abiding or uniform world adapted to minister to the development of morality, is a proposition the burden of proving which surely must be assigned to the opponent of theism. One can only say that in so far as we are enabled to pronounce on the matter by the experience we possess of the only world knowable to us, such proof would seem to be impossible. To illustrate what I mean here, I would remark that if water is to have the various properties which make it play the important part which that liquid does play in the economy of the physical world and the life of man, it cannot at the same time *not* have that noxious quality, the unpleasant capacity to drown us. The specific gravity of water is as much the necessary outcome of its molecular constitution as are its freezing-point and boiling-point; its thirst-quenching, cleansing, and all other beneficial characters. There cannot be assigned to any substance such as water an arbitrarily selected group of qualities, from which all that may happen to be unfortunate from man's point of view are eliminated, and yet the world, of which water forms an essential constituent, be a cosmos knowable and calculable by the physicist, or even the plain man. And similarly in all other cases. Mere determinateness—being this and not that—and com-

[3] *The Elements of Pain and Conflict in Human Life, Considered from a Christian Point of View*, p. 104. Published by The Cambridge University Press.

parative or absolute fixity of properties and behavior, involve such and such concatenations of qualities, and not others. Physical evils follow with the same necessity as physical good from that determination of the world-plan which secures that the world be a suitable stage for intelligent and moral life. The existence in the world of this form of evil, then, is no sign of lack of goodness or power in its Creator; it is simply a matter of compatibility of being and consistency of thought.

"If this be so, then the disadvantages which accrue from the determinateness and regularity of the physical world cannot be regarded as absolute or as superfluous evils. They are not absolute evils because they are part of the order which subserves the highest good of man, or provides opportunity for moral development; and they are not superfluous evils because they are the necessary outcome of that order. They are collateral effects of what in itself or as a whole is good because it is indispensable to the attainment of the highest good; they are necessary incidental consequences of an ordered, intelligible cosmos. They are not good; but they are 'good for,' rather than good for nothing."

But I think there is another viewpoint which helps. I think we may accept the view that the world, including the world of men and women, is not yet the world as God means it to be, but still, in a sense, a world in the making. "We see not yet all things subjected to him."[4] This is not what God dreamed of as his world, before the mass of swirling incandescent vapors broke away from the sun, sped through the abyss of space on its first journey, and then gradually cooling, shaping, forming, end-

[4] Hebrews c. 8.

lessly revolving in the awful loneliness of space, became the earth we love so much. God has not rested from his labors. He will not do things for us that we can do for ourselves, but he is ever urging, inspiring, leading men themselves to grapple with the family problem, and make his dreams come true.

And is the problem beyond us? I know how some of us feel when we stand beside the bed on which some young life is stretched out in an agony of pain. I know how tempted we are to rail against God. But supposing the great human family set itself to use all its resources to fight pain, I honestly believe that in ten years, *the amount of pain which constitutes a problem*—and we have seen that there is a minimum which is beneficial in warning us that something is wrong—could be exorcised from our midst.

If only we gave the doctors a chance, if we used all the power at our disposal to fight down sin, which brings such an awful entail of suffering to the innocent; if we used all our resources in controlling the machinery of our minds, practicing all the sane methods opened up for us under the magic word "psychology"; if, to the utmost, prayer, faith, intelligence, and money were poured forth in a grappling by the entire human family with the problem of suffering, I believe that in fifty years what remained would not constitute a problem at all. I believe that God's purpose lies in this direction. He will never do for us what we can do for ourselves, and we must not turn on him and saddle him with the responsibility of a problem with which we ourselves—as a family—are capable of dealing.

We must remember that the *measure* of the pain and suffering of the family is the *measure* of the Father's purpose, to cope with it and deal with it, bringing triumph both to God and man. This does not mean that the actual pain in the world is the will of God. We shall turn to that problem later. In a world like this, where free will and folly and ignorance operate, ten thousand things can happen to us which are not the will of God, but nothing can happen which it is beyond God's plan and purpose to redeem and use. The measure of suffering must be the measure of our faith, since it is the measure of God's all-beholding purpose. On no stage set otherwise could God reach the final act of the destiny of man. Not the actuality but the *possibility* of all the suffering we know was an essential in the working out of the human drama.

The thing that troubles many people is that the suffering of the innocent seems to be so utterly useless. Dimly the set of the world-stage can be seen to be good, but the suffering of the individual seems so insane and terrible as to have little cosmic value. The individual suffers without any obvious good to himself or to others. We think, for instance, of an innocent child who may be a victim of lust or cruelty, and we are tempted to say that in this as in many cases no conceivable final good can be worth the anguish we sometimes witness. I sympathize with those who watch their loved ones suffer and who say, "Nothing is worth the endurance of such agony;" but while I sympathize I feel that we speak thus because we see only in part, and I feel glad that Christ did not utter such words on Good Friday.

The only answer one can make is that if we had a complete knowledge of the universe, only then could we measure the value of the sufferings of the individual. But that suffering is related, in some way, to the universe.

I am afraid we must refrain even from trying to measure the one in terms of the other until our contemplation of both is complete and we can see things in their proper perspective.

I believe that all those who suffer are helping God redeem the world in at least two ways.

Firstly, their sufferings are stimulating inquiry and research, not only as to scientific means of prevention and cure on a material plane, but often by stimulating faith and prayer, which might be called scientific inquiry on the spiritual plane.

Miss Evelyn Underhill talks of "that redeeming prayer by which human spirits are called to work with God." She adds, concerning the saints: "Especially in its most mysterious reaches, in its redemptive, self-immolating action on suffering and sin, their intercession dimly reproduces and continues the supernatural work of Christ. Real saints do feel and bear the weight of the sins and pains of the world. It is the human soul's greatest privilege that we can thus accept redemptive suffering for one another—and they do."[5]

Secondly, all those who suffer, call forth sympathy and love from others, and if their suffering is obviously undeserved and unmerited, a greater sympathy and love is called forth than if it were deserved.

I should want to add, also, that although it is a speculation, I think one is thrust more and more to the belief that a redemption, unseen and unknown, and not able to be understood, is yet being brought about by the brave suffering of the innocent. If these three points could be fully appreciated, there could come, even in the hour of

[5] *Concerning the Inner Life*, p. 78. Methuen & Co., Ltd.

suffering, that deep joy which comes from sacrifice for others.

We must hold in mind that the solution of our problem must be found, as it were, within the painful experience. It is no solution to say, "Well, it will be over some day, and we must just live for that time." With the right perspective the saints have said with Von Hügel, "Suffering is the purest form of activity, perhaps the only form of activity." They have been able to say with Saint Ignatius, on his way to be torn to pieces, "Now I begin to be a disciple." They have been able to say with Jesus, "Now must the Son of man be glorified."

Yet there is more to be said, and, anticipating a later chapter, we may say four things in regard to God's relation to the suffering of the innocent.

1. He cannot prevent it without altering the whole basis of human life and rearranging it on a plan which would be far less good than the present one.

2. He is doing everything possible to remove the suffering of the innocent in a way consonant with those purposes, seen by him from the beginning of time, to be the best for the greatest number.

3. Though he did not send suffering upon the innocent personally, merely in order to teach the family great lessons, yet the growth of character in those who take the right attitude to pain, the influence such a bearing of pain has on those who watch, and the deepening of human sympathy, compassion, research, service, and love are undoubtedly inspired by God and are among the ways in which he is trying to bring his good out of the evil which the family, by its follies, refusals, ignorances, and sins, has brought on itself. It is hard to see how courage, utter self-sacrifice,

and the purest forms of heroism could develop without the possibility of suffering falling upon the least unworthy.

4. In regard to the remainder let us never forget that he bears his share. To rail against the suffering of the innocent is sometimes to forget that one rails against the greatest Sufferer. That well-beloved Son came to this family we call humanity. He became one of the family for better, for worse, for richer, for poorer, in sickness and in health. He took over the liabilities, though what he contributed was an asset the like of which no other member of the human family has ever brought to its highest wealth. In the prime of his manhood the sins of the family were visited on him. But when the blood beaded out from below the thorns on that majestic brow; when the lash fell, making great weals across that back; when rough iron nails tore through those hands so often lifted up in benediction and in healing; when the cross, bearing its quivering load, was lifted up and dropped with a sickening thud into the hole prepared for it, lacerating the wounds in hands and feet, there was no rebellion against the suffering of the innocent. Even the greatest sufferer can hardly but be silent before the greater suffering of the innocent Lamb of God.

The answer to our problem, from an intellectual point of view, lies, I think, as far as I can see an answer, in a careful consideration of the ideas set forth above. But from a spiritual point of view, we shall find heart satisfied, as well as intellect, only when in silent awe and wondering adoration, pleading to enter the fellowship of his sufferings, we kneel at the foot of the cross and kiss the feet of Him who hangs thereon, by whose stripes all his family shall at last be healed.

CHAPTER V

WHAT OF EARTHQUAKE, VOLCANO, AND STORM?

I AM writing this chapter on the morning when all the newspapers are full of the terrible earthquake that has taken place in the neighborhood of Quetta, when some thousands of people will be asking what the Christian has to say in the face of such a calamity. Thousands of our Indian friends will be telling themselves, that for some reason or other, God is angry. Thousands will believe that the present earthquake, like the last, is due to the fact that our airmen flew over the summit of Everest on a day that was unpropitious. We can get a little nearer to the truth than that, but probably nothing I shall be able to say in this chapter will answer the problem as we should like to have it answered.

The typhoon, the cyclone, the whirlwind, the earthquake, the volcanic eruption, the storm, which, in many instances, cannot possibly be foreseen, makes even serious thinkers wonder whether, as already suggested, a callous Fiend is on the throne of the universe, whether Anybody is on the throne of the universe at all, whether the universe has got out of hand, or whether it is badly made.

Following the assumptions of Chapter I, we may reiterate that God is good, and that God is all-powerful. Having contemplated the nature of God as revealed in Christ and the religious experience of the saints, we are bound to assume that even physical nature is a manifestation of God's character, and is working to some good end, concerning which we must be very patient and try to understand.

The suggestion that the universe is badly made has been seriously put forward. Let us look at it carefully. Lucretius[1] was bold enough to suggest a reconstruction of the universe on his own plan and to point out how much better things might have been if he had had the creative process in his hands. Lucretius scathingly criticized the physical conditions by which one zone is torrid and another frigid. He commented on the extent of barren sands and the waste of seas, on the prevalence of bad weather and storms, and on the abundance of poisonous plants and destructive animals.

Some philosophers said that by a slight change in the plane of the ecliptic, the fertility and climate of the earth could have been much improved, and that if the moon had been so placed as to revolve round the earth in the same time as that in which the earth revolves round the sun, she would have been always at the full and would have shone every night of the year.

Even John Stuart Mill,[2] as previously noted, deduced, from the maladjustments of the world, that its Author must be lacking in wisdom or goodness.

Dr. Griffith-Jones writes,[3] "One writer has declared that if a human optician were to blunder as badly as the supposed Author of eyes has done, he would be hissed out of his trade; for it is guilty of chromatic aberration, of spherical aberration, of possessing a blind spot right in its center, of needless radiation of the light, of a shadow

[1] Bk. 2, Par. 77, to Bk. 5, Par. 196.
[2] *Three Essays on Religion*, pp. 28-31.
[3] *Providence*, Vol. I, p. 140.

cast on the retina by the clumsy arrangement of its blood-vessels, and of the imperfect sensitiveness of the yellow spot which is the actual center of vision."

Of course all that has been singled out for denunciation is exceptional. Scientists agree that the creation on the whole is of amazing unity, showing the marks of the most amazing skill and forethought. I feel, then, that the Christian can claim that in view of the orderliness of creation, down to the smallest detail, say of the body of a worm, or the instinct of an ant, it may well be that these alleged maladjustments are just as purposive and have uses and functions which we do not yet understand.

For instance, later scientists have shown that if the plane of the ecliptic of the moon had been altered in the way Lucretius desired, the whole mechanism of the solar system would have been thrown into disorder; that if the moon had been made to revolve, as Comte and Laplace suggested, we should have had only one sixteenth of the moonlight we now enjoy; and that, further, the moon would have been in constant danger of extinction and there would have been no tides.

Concerning the construction of the eye, later scientists have condemned this imperfection as an optical lens, but have pointed out that it is not meant to be a scientific instrument but an organ of vision; that each animal normally possesses that efficiency of vision most suitable for its own vital purpose, and that while so-called imperfections would be troublesome in an artificially constructed lens, the adaptation of the eye to its function is complete and that this is seen in the very limits which are set to its defects.

It is worth quoting Doctor Martineau here, for in his

Study of Religion[4] he definitely sets out to answer the poet Lucretius. He says: "The Roman poet, it seems, would have preferred a human estate all under culture, compact and occupied, uniform in temperature, and with no more water than was needful for irrigation and for drink; with no moor and fountain to part the fields, no freshening play of ocean and air where man is not, no refrigerating winds to fling a wreath of snow, no African glow to cross over and move the Alpine glaciers; but a snug little planet, without a waste place or a wild beast, and so comfortable that it would soon swarm like a Chinese empire or an ant-hill, and 'no one could be alone in all the earth.' This is the landscape-gardening of philosophy, from which for my part I gladly escape back to the wild forest or the open sea, or even the stern wonders of the icebergs and the northern lights. On Comte's proposal for improving the moon by having it full every night, I could pass no mathematical judgment; his scientific critics say it would be fatal to the planet's equilibrium; but I confess to such a love of the monthly story of the orb from the first crescent to the last descrescent phase, that, to save it, I would accept a gaslight, or even carry a lantern on dark nights."

In the same way Doctor Martineau deals with Darwin's criticism of the nature of the sting of the bee. Darwin sarcastically pointed out that the bee's sting is so made that its use, when it stings a person, causes its own death by tearing out its viscera. Doctor Martineau shows that this is a case of the misapplication of a tool meant originally as a drill for cutting grooves in wood, which, in moments of madness, the bee turns into a weapon of

[4] Vol. I, p. 354.

attack. Probably, in the course of time, natural selection will end, either in eliminating the perverted instinct to sting, or else equipping the bee with a different weapon. Here we see a tiny illustration of the point that the world is a world in the making, and in the sting of the bee we are watching a weapon the fashioning of which is not yet finished.

The conclusion, therefore, of our first point I think is this. That in spite of what appear to be defects in the ordering of nature and the construction of the world, the universe, not yet finished, has been planned by a Mind of infinite power and infinite goodness for the greatest good of the greatest number; and if there comes what we call calamity, God is able to justify it in ways which, as yet, we cannot understand.

But beyond all this we may notice some other points which help us in our study of calamity.

Take, for example, the terrible havoc that has been wrought by volcanoes and earthquakes. So dreadful has this havoc been that it is not surprising that men feel that their faith in God is almost shattered by it. Yet we have to try to understand that there are many things in life which we accept as good which are due to the very same laws which make the earthquake and volcanoes possible. The safety and stability of the house in which I write these words depend on the laws which make the earthquake. In his book *Volcanoes,* Professor J. W. Judd, of the Royal School of Mines, writes as follows: "The first impression produced upon the mind when the phenomena of volcanic action are studied, is that we have here exhibitions of destructive violence, the effects of which must be entirely mischievous and disastrous to the living beings on the earth's surface. A little consideration, however, will convince us that the grand and terrible displays of volcanic energy have given rise to exaggerated assertions concerning their destructive effects. Internal forces continually at work within the earth's crust, perform a series of most important functions in connection with the economy of the globe; and were the actions of these forces to die out, our planet would soon cease to be fit for the habitation of living beings. By the admirable balancing of external and internal forces on our own globe, the conditions necessary to animal and vegetable existence are almost constantly maintained, and thus, interruptions of such conditions which are produced by hurricanes and floods, or by volcanic outbursts and earthquakes, may safely be regarded as the insignificant accidents of what is on the whole a very perfectly working piece of machinery."

In some cases one feels that man's foolishness in building large stone structures on ground which he knows is liable to earthquake shock is responsible for most of what is called calamity in the time of disaster. Dr. T. Nakamura, Professor of Architecture at Tokyo University, was sent out by the Japanese government for the purpose of examining the facts of the San Francisco earthquake. In his report he used this remarkable sentence: "Dishonest mortar was responsible for nearly all the earthquake damage in San Francisco."

According to the London *Times,* the appalling destruction in Quetta City is traced to the poor constructional quality of the buildings. Although Quetta was known to be in a serious earthquake zone, little appears to have been done in the city to counteract the devastation of earthquakes by sound building methods. In Japan, California, New Zealand, and other regions where earthquakes occur efforts have been made in recent years to avert the collapse of buildings by the erection of earthquake-proof structures; but Quetta, with foreknowledge of its likely fate, appears to have neglected this safeguard. Such earthquake-proof buildings as had been built in the area survived the catastrophe. In the railway lines, where enormous damage was done and casualties were heavy, *earthquake-proof buildings remained intact.*[5] Not even their chimneys fell.

I am not trying to pretend that all the horror caused by volcano and earthquake is due to man's foolishness, but we are bound, first of all, to exclude those human elements in catastrophe before we begin to arraign God on a charge of making his universe badly or carelessly, or having no regard to our pains and sorrows. He has admittedly put us into a hard school, but we must be much more ready to learn his lessons. Until we do, the horror will be greater and the suffering more poignant. And again and again happenings which seem to be entirely an act of God have a human factor behind them. Part of the great human family has been foolish or ignorant or sinful and has not used its resources.

I have already referred in these pages to the vast desert wastes. Criticism, it will be remembered, was made of a God who left vast areas of the world barren, desert wastes. But is God wholly responsible for this? In reading the story of Mr. Kennedy Shaw's recent journeys in *Dead Libya* nothing is clearer than the fact that what is now desert waste was once a fertile region carrying the vast

[5] Italics mine.

populations of ancient civilization. Explorers tell us that no climatic change is responsible for the fact that fertile land has become a desert. "Timgad in N. Africa, for example, and the sister city, Lambrèse, were busy and populous centers in Roman days, and there is no evidence of any catastrophic change of climate since that time." The stark fact is that man's lack of foresight and bad management are entirely responsible for the existence of the vast deserts. Man has exploited the soil, deprived it of trees, burned off the vegetation, overgrazed the herbage. The soil has become reduced in quality, has powdered and become unable to retain moisture. During the dry season powdering of the surface takes place and surface soil is caught up by winds and swept away. During heavy rains soil is washed away and loses its valuable soluble salts. Fertility was gradually lost through man's mismanagement. In parts of the world where soil is continuously damp this loss of fertility is not serious, but in those areas where there are torrential downpours and scorching winds the loss of fertility is serious enough to be alarming. South Africa and parts of Australia and Canada might be mentioned as examples. "Valuable agricultural land in French and British Nigeria and in the French Sudan is being conquered and absorbed by the Sahara Desert at a rate estimated to exceed a kilometer a year." "Dr. O. E. Baker, a leading American authority on economic geography, has estimated that since America was settled, an area has been denuded of its surface soil equal to the area of cultivated land in Germany." It was to protect the Middle West from the menace we are describing that President Roosevelt proposed to plant a belt of trees a thousand miles long and a hundred broad. One American expert declares that unless there is a drastic change in the way the soil is now treated, the U.S.A. has left to it "less than one hundred years of virile national existence."

In the Mesopotamian campaign during the Great War we lost far more men through the climate than through Turkish bullets. Men who were killed by sunstroke and through the dangerous climate were often regarded as having been struck down by what is called "an act of God." But one wonders whether it is fair to think thus when one remembers what has happened. When the Turks conquered Mesopotamia, they taxed the trees. The Arab thereupon cut down all the trees unless the fruit of the tree would pay for the tax. The fact that so much vegetation has disappeared in Mesopotamia is the most significant factor in accounting for the climate. If, therefore, man has entirely altered the climate of Mesopotamia and other areas of the world, as seems to have been the case, he can hardly call it an act of God if the climate brings subsequent sunstroke or other disasters which at first do not appear to be the result of human folly.

Another point I think might be made. In very many cases of catastrophe wonderful good has followed. It is, of course, difficult and perhaps impossible to measure the good against the evil. But suppose death turned out not to be the kind of calamity we so often think it, then is it wild to say that the death of a large number of victims of calamity is not too high a price to pay for the changed ideas of the survivors? I can no longer regard death as a terrible disaster when I realize how prone man is to it through the operation of the forces in the universe.

One of the hardest things to change in India is the rigid

caste system which has been in vogue for centuries. The Brahmin is the highest caste of all. Recently in Quetta a Brahmin who had been crushed under the ruins of his house had had his leg amputated at the thigh, and had for several days been lying in hospital, with a British orderly to look after him and others. One day he asked for the chaplain, to whom he said: "All my life I have been what you might call a religious man. But the work I have seen done in this hospital is the most godlike thing I have ever seen done by man for man."[6] How many sacrificed lives is such a change of mind worth?

When the great Japanese earthquake took place, the nations of the world rushed to help Japan, and it is said that the earthquake meant a greater step forward in the brotherhood of other nations with Japan than a century of unclouded progress. We begin to love those whom we are moved to help; and not only did outside nations help Japan, but her own princes lavishly spent their fortunes for the poor. The community forgot for the time their ancient animosities because of the common need. Again and again it is difficult to see how any happening could produce such progress, socially, nationally and internationally, as what was called a calamity did in fact propose, but in balancing good and evil we may say that those who suffered in such a calamity might well be thought of as dying for their country, since their death, and the shock it brought, made new friendships for Japan and the building of a new Tokyo.

"It is clear from experience," says Doctor D'Arcy,[7] "that true progress, and victory over all that we sum up as

---

[6] *The Times* (London), July 2, 1935.
[7] *Providence and the World Order*, p. 241. Hodder & Stoughton.

evil, can only be attained by painful struggle." "Only by education and discipline," says the same writer in another place,[8] "can men be brought to overcome their selfish inclinations for the good of the whole. And this education and discipline involve pain. Here, surely, is the place of pain in the moral history of mankind."

One of the points which we shall have occasion to reiterate again and again is that God has put us into a stern school. As Matthew Arnold says,

> "Earthquakes do not scorn
> The just man to entomb,
> Nor lightning stand aside
> To find his virtues room."

Every one of us could illustrate the idea behind that terrible fact. Dr. E. Stanley Jones's book called *Christ and Human Suffering* is full of illustrations which move one to the depths. I read one which specially impressed me. Doctor Jones says:[9] "Today I picked up my letters with eagerness to find out about my daughter's graduation from high school in the Himalayas, an event I had reluctantly to miss because of my China tour. After describing the happy event it told of the trip down the mountains toward their homes in the plains—an event always full of gaiety and bubbling happiness. But not this one! For one of the girls, who also had graduated, turned to wave good-by to some of her companions on the hills above, stepped backward against a low wall, so she thought, but it proved to be an open space in the wall,

---

[8] *God and the Struggle for Existence*, p. 27. Student Christian Movement Press, Ltd.
[9] P. 16. The Abingdon Press.

and down she fell two hundred feet to her death. And she was a widowed mother's only daughter."

I was deeply touched by the story of a little boy who, running home from school, was struck dead by lightning in the center of a field. I did not then know that an open field was a place of danger. If the little chap had been sheltering under a tree, the blow would have been easier to bear. One's mind would argue, then, that he should have been taught that a tree may conduct electricity and that it is always a dangerous shelter in a thunderstorm, and one could have put down the calamity to ignorance; but the little chap was doing nothing he knew to be foolish, doing nothing that one could call human folly or sin; and one wonders what the parents made of the death of their little child under such circumstances.

Yet that sad death taught me and thousands of others that an open field in a thunderstorm is dangerous. The very next day the press, which is one of the greatest teachers in modern civilization, and the advantages of which can hardly be exaggerated, told the public to avoid (1) small sheds and shelters if in exposed location, (2) isolated trees, (3) wire fences, (4) hilltops and *wide open spaces.*

I think it is no exaggeration to say that that little fellow gave his life for others. His parents, and, indeed, all of us, must think of him with honor as we think of those who by dying bring knowledge which saves others. For thus in the hard school of life lessons are learned, knowledge is added to the family store. We learn at the cost of another's pain. Everywhere man is up against the stern fight to subdue nature to his will; and in reality the problem is the same whether one person is overwhelmed by avalanche or storm, or twenty thousand engulfed by an earthquake.

I have already referred to the fallacy of regarding natural calamities as divine judgments (p. 33). In order to place natural calamities in the right perspective we must cease thinking of them as sent by a wise Providence as a means of arousing a wicked and indifferent world to a realization of the power and righteousness of God.

I have a reference in my notebook to an ancient sermon preached in 1756 in which the preacher states that when God finds that pain, sickness, loss, bereavement, and disappointment, which the preacher calls the "usual scourges of the Divine Hand," do not serve to waken his children to a needful sense of God's power, then "the Universal Ruler departs from his usual methods of chastisement and uses external executioners of his vengeance which are generally these four—famine, sword, pestilence, and earthquake."

A correspondent informs me that John Wesley's sermon on "The Cause and Cure of Earthquakes" was published in 1750, and that in it he affirms that earthquakes are a sign of God's anger against sin. The very word "pain" comes from the Greek word πόινή, meaning "punishment." The view was long held, thousands hold it now, but fortunately the sway of this idea over thoughtful minds is gradually losing its hold.

Again and again we find evidences that the natural calamity is not a divine judgment. In many an Indian village it happens that the mission building has been smashed and the brothel is left standing. The home of the humble Christian is destroyed and a gambling hell is left intact.

We can only conclude that all things are working to a divine end worthy of the risks taken; that while we may not call this world-in-the-making the best of all possible worlds, it is the world of best possibilities, and that God is willing to sacrifice us and himself to get a greater good out of every calamitous happening than is possible without the possibility of such sacrifice.

The truth that is going to keep us steady and our heart quiet is that behind these natural calamities which terrify us is not a mere vast, blind Force, but a God, and, moreover, a God who does not think in masses, though these huge calamities might lead us to think he does. He still has an unbroken plan for the individual, though individuals in thousands are engulfed through volcanic eruption or earthquake shock.

We deceive ourselves by measuring suffering in terms of the number of people who suffer. The *problem* is not bigger if thirty thousand are engulfed by earthquake than if only one suffers. We cannot usefully add together all cases of suffering as if the *problem* were thus made more difficult.

It is quite open to the cynic or the skeptic or the agnostic to pile up facts against any idea of Providence or purpose; and, quite honestly, it must be admitted that the evidences are strong enough to break down the faith of those who have not thought things through. But let your mind contemplate alternatives! Listen to the poet Zangwill. He expresses what many have come to accept:

> "Thy nymphs are gone, the fairies flown:
> The ancient gods forever fled;
> The stars are silent overhead;

The music of the spheres is still;
The night is dark, the wind is chill;
The later gods have followed Pan,
And Man is left alone with Man."

Listen to another poet expressing another modern point of view:

"We must play the game with a careless smile
Though there's nothing in the hand;
We must toil as if it were worth our while
Spinning our ropes of sand;
And laugh and cry, and live and die
At the waft of an Unseen Hand."

And then listen to two other poets. Here is Alfred Norris:

"*You* see a world that wildly whirls
Through coiling clouds and battle smoke,
And drenched with blood the children's curls
And women's hearts by thousands broke.

"I see a host above it all,
Where angels wield their conquering sword;
And thrones may rise, and thrones may fall,
But comes the Kingdom of the Lord."

And then listen to Tennyson's faith:

"That nothing walks with aimless feet;
That not one life shall be destroyed
Or cast as rubbish to the void,
When God hath made the pile complete;

"That not a worm is cloven in vain;
That not a moth with vain desire
Is shriveled in a fruitless fire,
Or but subserves another's gain.

"Behold, we know not anything;
I can but trust that good shall fall
At last—far off—at last, to all,
And every winter change to spring."

"So runs my dream. . . ."

For myself, with the problem thought through as far as I can think it, I can only express my faith in the great words of Saint Paul, "To them that love God all things work together for good."

Let me finish the chapter with an imaginative picture. A man is seated on a height overlooking the city of Tokyo ruined by earthquake. He is a man highly respected, looked up to and honored by his fellow citizens. His wife and children have perished in the disaster. His home has fallen in ruins; his business has been burned to the ground. He himself has been injured and has barely escaped with his life. Overcome with complete mental and physical exhaustion he falls asleep and dreams. In his dream it seems that his wife and children come to him, hand in hand. They are radiantly happy, and though through all his future days he could never remember all they said, he never forgot that they spoke of death as just the passing through a gateway, the last splendid adventure of life. He was not to grieve for them, they told him, but wait contentedly till the great angel should set him free to come to them. His first glimpse of this angel, they told him, would be the shadows underneath her wings, but when she touched him, he would see the quiet beauty of her tender, glorious face.

But a more wonderful impression than this lived with the man through all the years. It seemed in his dream that his wife spoke to him of a vision she had been allowed to see of their dear, dear city, built anew, fairer than ever, its squalidness gone, its hatreds gone, its selfishness gone, its spirit praised by all men; a city cleansed by suffering, strengthened by new ties of brotherhood, spreading outward to make a new Japan, a new world. "But it will remain a vision," she had said, "unless you go and help to build it."

The man awoke, and, wakening, muttered to himself, "A new and nobler city, out of all this blood and tears and ruin; is it possible?" And there came to his mind words which he had never understood before; words which he had read in Christian writings about "a holy city . . . coming down out of heaven from God," and a voice that said, "Behold, I make all things new." And the man rose to his feet, turned away, and went slowly down the hill. Heart and brain were on fire with this new, tremendous purpose which God had given him to do. The words he had heard were strange and obscure no longer. Now he understood.

CHAPTER VI

IS SUFFERING THE WILL OF GOD?

SUFFERING is either the will of God or it is not. This is the dilemma that has harassed many minds for long and bitter years. If it is not, many argue that their lives are in the hands of fate or chance. A good many Easterners accept the idea of pure chance; and having had some of these folk as friends I must say there is a healthy, open-air, if pagan, attitude which can take even a hard blow as just "a bit of bad luck," just the blow of chance. I hasten to say that I do not think this position can be reasonably defended, but it is probably healthier and less morbid in its effects than the bad thinking of many people in our churches, who, as soon as anything in the nature of suffering befalls them, search introspectively for some sin for which the suffering might be regarded as a punishment. One of the greatest sorrows of any minister's life is to find after he has been preaching about the nature of God to a congregation for several years, that a man, whom he thought had his thinking anchored in reality, has not progressed beyond the point where he supposes that he has gone bankrupt, not because he was a poor business man or because his debtors did not pay up, or because his partner was a fool or a knave, but because he himself had not been saying his prayers lately. It is astonishing to find how quick is the tendency to suppose that any kind of calamity is, as it were, handed out as punishment for a supposed sin. In the same way when a mother loses her baby, instead of supposing that it is because the doctor's knowledge and skill were not adequate to the situation, or a nurse was careless, or the illness not noticed in time to be adequately treated, or that the child suffered because the knowledge of the conditions of illness was not great enough to prevent death, the tender-hearted mother will lash her soul into torture by trying to make her mind believe that God has taken her baby to teach her a lesson, and that the death of the child is a punishment inflicted upon her, say, for not going to church lately. One of the things I hope to do in this chapter is at least to smash that kind of thinking.

I should wish my readers, in the first place, not to dismiss the Eastern idea of fate or luck as though it were a conception of life which contained no valuable grain of truth. Cut out, of course, any thought that there can be effect without adequate cause, or that the cosmos of order ever gives place to the chaos of chance. Cut out all thought of luck in the sense that a mascot can bring good fortune, or that a charm can prevent illness.[1] But leave room in your estimate for things that happen, not because God may will these things but owing to the fact that life is intermingled in a way which cannot possibly be foreseen by us or intended by God. Every human personality has free will which can be misused or, not to use so strong a word, used carelessly and thoughtlessly, and the stage on which we have to play our parts is one that is largely

[1] Save, of course, that in the case of very suggestible people the set of the mind is important. If the charm is believed in, it may make the wearer exclude the thought of illness and believe that his health is being guarded. Such a belief often increases resistance to infection, especially in relation to certain illnesses. The advice to carry a potato in the pocket would long ago have passed to the limbo of absurdities had there not been this grain of wheat in the chaff. Curiously enough, some rheumatoid conditions are strangely amenable to suggestion. A friend of mine, highly cultured and well known in public life, never leaves home without carrying in his pocket a small potato!

unknown. By this I mean that we are in a universe where man learns very, very slowly. He not only sins willfully, but, for lack of knowledge, he acts foolishly. On such a stage and with such personalities operating, although nothing happens without a cause and nothing happens without the knowledge of God, yet ten thousand things can happen through the crisscross of free-will action and the interaction of factors not yet brought under our knowledge and foresight and understanding.

A little while ago, after heavy rain, the dripping of water in some way soaked through the insulation of two electric wires and caused a doorbell to ring in the middle of the night. A woman, alone in the house, hearing the bell ring, went to the bedroom door and opened it. Her movement, crossing the floor, apparently loosened the door of a wardrobe behind her which contained a mirror. The door swung open, the mirror reflected the light of a street lamp and rotated the reflection from behind the woman across the landing outside the bedroom door. The woman deduced immediately that the light was the flash of a burglar's lamp and the ringing bell a police-summons. Panic followed, and she fell in a faint on the floor with rather serious physical hurt as well as mental shock. Here is an illustration of suffering which one could almost call accidental. It is difficult to put one's finger on the ignorance, folly, or sin of man which caused it. It is impossible to believe that God intended it, or, in fact, to blame anybody at all. The suffering must be put down to the unfortunate result of intermingling factors which are part of the make-up of the universe. We might be justified in calling such suffering a sheer bit of bad luck.

It may be necessary to point out more clearly that there cannot be any such thing as chance if by chance, or luck, is meant an effect without a cause. If we knew all the factors operating in any situation, then no resultant would be capable of causing surprise. If I knew all the laws and conditions governing the tossing up of a penny, I could determine with accuracy whether it would come down heads or tails. But in the present extent of human knowledge many resultants are bound to be uncertain.

A paragraph may be added to point out that although God knows the resultant of all the intermingling of the factors we have mentioned, that does not make such a resultant his will, nor does his knowledge cause that particular resultant to happen. If I knew all the complexes in another's mind, all the motives, ideals, and desires, the resistances and resources in another's life, I should be able to say, with something approaching certainty, what that person would do under any given set of circumstances. If my knowledge were complete, my certainty would be complete. Yet it is not my knowledge which produces his behavior. It is the sum of his complexes acted upon by his free will and choice, and the responsibility is his. God knows what I am going to do every hour for the rest of my life, but it is not his knowing that forces me to the doing. The factors which make up my decision reside within myself. The matter might be put more simply by saying that if I open my study door and hold out a luscious bone to a starving dog in the hall, I "know" that he will move toward the bone, unless there is some more attractive goal elsewhere. But it is not my knowing that makes him move toward the bone. It is his hunger.

Some people torture themselves by the thought that because God knows what is going to happen to them, events are bound to happen thus; but his knowing is not the causative factor. He knows the end to which those causative factors will lead. The philosophers would tell us that although we speak of past and present and future, and say that God knows what will happen to us in twenty years' time, those conceptions of time are concessions to our limited human way of thinking of reality, and that it would be truer to say that, to God, the events of the next twenty years have already happened, or perhaps more correctly, are happening. What we view as past, present, and future he views as an eternal present. We really must try to break from the tyranny of a mistaken idea that we are bound in a rigid system of destiny simply because God is omniscient. He knows what I did with my free will in the past. Yet in regard to the past I find it easy to admit that his knowing did not compel my doing. It is just as easy for God to know what I shall do with my free will in the future. But his knowing no more compels my doing in the future than it did in the past.

In my work as chaplain at a hospital in a large city I remember the case of a man who had cancer of the eye. The agony through which he passed made me a convinced believer in euthanasia.[2] The injection of morphia only seemed to give him relief for a shorter and shorter time. I used to go to see him quite frequently, and I

[2] By euthanasia is meant the deliberate putting out of their sufferings by "easy death" such patients as would otherwise linger for a long period in the agony of painful and incurable disease. Reform is needed here. At present the law would punish anyone who put a human being out of severe agony and anyone who kept a dog in it.

can recall now sitting on his bed, my hand sore with the intensity of his grip when waves of pain passed over him. In spite of much that has been written on God chastening his children, I simply cannot believe that that man's suffering was the will of God in the sense in which the words are usually used. I cannot believe a thing is true about God for which a man, could he bring such anguish to another's life, would be in jail or in a lunatic asylum. Jesus said, "If ye then, being evil, know how to give good gifts unto your children, how much more shall your heavenly Father . . . ?" When men asked what God was like, Jesus commonly told them to think of an ideal earthly father. Supposing it to be within his power, what earthly father would give his little child cancer of the eye?

If it is pointed out that God is responsible for the lightning which strikes a man down, and that no man would be allowed so to strike another were it within his power to do so, I want to point out the essential difference between believing that God sends specific disease, *intending* the individual to suffer anguish as punishment for something done, and believing that God has put us into a universe where dangerous factors operate which, through our ignorance, folly, or sin, may bring suffering to us. It is one thing to take a man by main force and thrust him between the rollers of some huge machine in an engineering shop. It is another thing to give him a job in the engineering shop where there is dangerous machinery in which he may get cut up and mangled if he does not know how to work the machinery, if he is careless or foolish, or if a fellow workman pushes him—through folly or sin—against unguarded wheels. If I give my boy a pair of roller skates, I immediately make it possible for him to get a bad bump. That is a very different thing from taking him by the neck and banging his head upon the ground.

The more I think of punishment in the universe, the more it seems to me that God's penalties are not, as it were, handed out to the individual. They are included in the scheme of things, and the individual suffers for the family.

A parent may sometimes punish a child by means brought in from without the situation, such as the infliction of pain. But a wise parent finds that his ideal way of imposing discipline is to have a state of things in his home in which naughtiness brings its own deprivation, sin its own punishment. I feel that God has so made the universe that his penalties are not brought in from without. Sin involves its own penalty and wickedness its own punishment. The penalty of lust, for instance, is that a man can be satisfied with lust; and the penalty of avarice is that a man can be satisfied with money until God opens his eyes to all that he has missed. And this is a different understanding of the phrase, "It is the will of God," from that which is popularly associated with the words.

It does not mean, to reiterate, that God hands out a cancer because a man has been lustful. It means that man is put into a universe in which he slowly and surely discovers that life will only work out successfully in one way, and that is God's way. Just as I may give my boy roller skates and thus provide him with new pleasure, but also with new possibilities of suffering, so God has given me my free will, my slowly working mind, my share in the family blessings, because all those things are, in his sight, very good. He knows—and it is his will that it is so—that that free will, so precious to me because my virtue, such as it is, is not mechanical but chosen, may, if it is misused, bring me into a hell of pain. He has given me my slowly working mind so that I experience the thrilling joy of new discoveries, knowing perfectly well that, while I am still ignorant, my ignorance may bring me terrible suffering, and he gives me my share in the family blessings which, in an earlier chapter, we saw to be such a privilege (p. 68), knowing that he who shares the family assets must share the family liabilities too. He does not will these sufferings in the sense of intending them, but in order that I may win the joy he wants me to have, he is putting me into a universe where such sufferings are possible.

Take the boy with the roller skates again. While he is ignorant he may suffer many falls. If he acts foolishly with them, he may suffer. Further, to enjoy skating where others skate means that others may bump into him. As the donor of the skates I *will* none of these calamities. I only will conditions in which they are possible.

Let the reader think of the calamities in his own life and then assess how many of them come from ignorance or folly or sin, not his own, perhaps, but from his membership of the great human family, and then let him remember that God's will is to replace ignorance with knowledge, folly with wisdom, and sin with holiness. He will then, I think, understand what I mean by saying that none of these calamities which come from ignorance, folly or sin can be looked upon as the will of God in the sense that, as isolated events, they were his intention. It wrings one's heart to hear a woman saying, "Why did God let my baby die?" or to hear a dear friend say, "Why does my loved one suffer so?" or to hear a mother say, "Why was my boy killed in the war?" We must try to be brave enough to sit down quietly and think things through, and then we shall find that God did not intend them. He put his children into a school where such things might happen. And God has not finished with the baby or the loved one or the soldier boy; but he could not have prevented the calamities without a denial of those principles of the universe which, as far as we can see, are the best on which such a universe could be run.

Perhaps we can get a little further if we pursue the analogy between suffering and sin. No one can suppose that God wills sin, but he allows sin. If he did not allow sin, he could not allow free will, and if he did not allow free will, then we should be mere automata. We should not choose good because it was good. We should be good because we could not be anything else. Indeed, the words "good," "choice," "morality," and "virtue," would have no meaning. Therefore God has willed conditions which make sin possible and must be said to be responsible for the fact that there could be such a thing as sin in the world. Yet, again, no one could say, honestly, when a man sins that it is the will of God. I think we shall come to see that the analogy is fairly close; that God does not will suffering, but that he could not achieve his own higher purposes if he made a universe from which all possibility of suffering were excluded. He is therefore responsible for the fact that there is such a thing as suffering. Yet no one could say of any particular bit of suffering, "This is the will of God."

Now go back to the question of sin. When a man sins, he does not go on the scrap-heap as a failure. There is such a thing as forgiveness and restoration. God can use even a man's sins. I need not stay here to point out the danger behind that statement. Saint Paul dealt with it finally in the letter to the Romans.[8] Similarly, when the individual suffers, that is not the end of God's dealings with him. His suffering can be used. It can become redemptive, as we shall see. God is never ultimately defeated by it.

We are so frequently muddled in our thinking about the will of God because we think of God as though he were perfectly free to act as we should want to act if we had unlimited magical power suddenly thrust upon us. As we bend over the cot of a suffering little child we imagine what we should do if we had the power which God is often supposed to have. If the reader still thinks thus, I must press him to go back and read again the first chapter of this book. I think he may then see that, in a real sense, God is conditioned by his self-imposed limitations and also that if he broke those self-imposed limitations—supposing that were possible—the universe which resulted would be far harder to understand and far less satisfactory than we ourselves can see this one to be. We are so apt to isolate God from the universe and isolate an event from its complex setting, and torture ourselves by wondering why the isolated God does not act upon the iso-

[8] Romans 6. 15.

lated event, when, in fact, neither isolation is possible or intelligible.

It may be necessary here to say a word to those who believe that if we tell them their suffering is not the will of God, we are depriving them of a measure of comfort. "Tell me it is God's will that I should suffer this," says a patient, "and I can stand it. But tell me that it is not God's will and God cannot help it, and I am lost." I would not take from such a patient the sense of comfort he gains by thinking thus if I thought there were any final comfort in thinking falsely; but I feel certain that there is far more comfort in thinking with Jesus than in thinking that our pain is God's intention.

How can anybody read the Gospels and suppose that the victims whom Jesus healed were suffering because it was the will of God they should suffer? Were the healing acts of Jesus, then, contrary to the will of God? In Luke 13. 1-5 we read these words: "There were present at that season some that told him of the Galileans, whose blood Pilate had mingled with their sacrifices. And Jesus answering said unto them, Suppose ye that these Galileans were sinners above all the Galileans, because they suffered such things? I tell you, Nay: but, except ye repent, ye shall all likewise perish. Or those eighteen, upon whom the tower in Siloam fell, and slew them, think ye that they were sinners above all men that dwelt in Jerusalem? I tell you, Nay." Here is a definite denial that the calamity of the martyred Galileans, or the victims on whom the tower of Siloam fell, were killed because they had sinned more than others. "Suffering," says Jesus, "is not punishment." I feel that that ought to end, forever, the worry of anybody who supposes that suffering is the will of God in the sense that it is handed out as a punishment for sin.

Turn to verse 16 of the same chapter, where Jesus refers to a woman "being a daughter of Abraham *whom Satan hath bound* these eighteen years." Without going into the question of whether Jesus believed in a personal devil or whether his reference to Satan meant "the sum-total influence of all the evil inclinations and errors of customs and false ideas which have originated within the mind of man," it is obvious that Jesus definitely thinks this poor woman's suffering was not the will of God, but was the result of forces definitely regarded as evil. "Suffering," says Jesus, "is not the hand of God laid upon you but the hand of evil."

When we turn to the well-known passage in John 9. 2, I think we find further evidence that Jesus did not regard suffering as due to sin either in the sufferer or in his parents. One of the most dangerous things we can do is to contemplate a person's suffering and decide that it is due to his sin or that of his parents. If I may adopt a new punctuation which I have quoted elsewhere, the passage reads like this: As Jesus "passed by, he saw a man blind from his birth. And his disciples asked him, saying, Rabbi, who did sin, this man, or his parents, that he should be born blind? Jesus answered, Neither did this man sin, nor his parents, but that the works of God should be made manifest in him. I must work the works of him that sent me while it is day. The night cometh when no man can work." If this punctuation be allowed, we find that Jesus' answer amounts to this: "One thing is quite clear: this man's blindness is not due to his sin or to that of his parents. And it is useless to speculate exactly why he should have been born blind." (Jesus recognizes how rarely suffering falls on the guilty parties or their immediate relatives and how rarely the amount of suffering bears a quantitative relation to the supposed fault.) "What we have to do," says Jesus, "instead of useless speculations, is to work the works of God in order that he, and all those like him, may find relief." In other words, the works of God must be *made manifest in him;* and such manifestation is called health.

I find a certain sympathy with the passionate cry of Mr. Britling in H. G. Wells' famous novel, "Why, if I thought there was a God who looked down on battles and death and all the horror of this war, able to prevent these things . . . I would spit in his empty face." Nor, I think, is it enough to say that suffering can produce in men fortitude, patience, and other virtues. Suffering has in it that *possible* value but not that *inevitable* value. It has a possible disciplinary value but not an inevitable disciplinary value, for often it leads to rebellion, bitterness, and despair. The idea that suffering is essential to the virtues contains truth, but the statement fails to cover significant facts unless stated differently. What are we to make of those who are born insane? And what are we to make of the amount of suffering which does not bring any good? I plead that we should cease to think that God sends these things. He does not send a germ of typhoid to your home any more than he sends a tiger to a village. People are frequently so inconsistent in their thinking about pain, suffering, and the will of God, that if a patient dies, they will say, "Well, it is the will of

God," and the next minute they will be telling one that if a certain surgeon could have been procured, the patient undoubtedly would have lived. One cannot charge them with being illogical. They are in no mood for argument. But the logic of the situation would seem to be that a skillful surgeon can outwit the will of God. I prefer to think that a skillful surgeon *does* the will of God.

Here I want to quote Principal Cairns. "Jesus," he says, "seems to have felt toward physical and mental disease precisely as every good modern physician feels toward it. In this respect he does not differ from the ordinary medical standpoint, nor can we understand him unless we appreciate this. He always assumes that disease is part of the kingdom of evil, and never once does he give the slightest sign to the contrary. Not only does he try to heal all who are brought to him, but he sends his disciples forth with a general commission to heal indiscriminately. His unvarying assumption, where there are failures, is that there has not been enough faith either on the part of the healers or of the sick or their friends and neighbors. His underlying idea can only be that God is always on the side of health rather than of disease, and that where the latter triumphs, something is as it ought not to be."[4]

We ought, therefore, to conclude that where suffering exists it is the will of God that it should go, but that God's will cannot be done for various reasons, all of which are on man's side. For his comfort in such a case, the sufferer must trust in an omnipotence that can bring person-

[4] *His Life and Ours*, pp. 250-51. The Abingdon Press. *Discipleship*, pp. 104ff. The Abingdon Press.

ality ultimately to the goal of God's final purpose, and the patient must do what he can to turn his sufferings into the golden asset which we shall describe in a later chapter.

The question of the cross is too big for us here, and I have discussed it elsewhere.[5] In brief, perhaps we may say here that there is a true sense in which the crucifixion was no more the will of God than any other murder in history for which man was responsible. We cannot suppose the will of those who plotted Christ's death and the will of God were the same thing. I do not mean by this, of course, that the cross was a kind of accident which was outside God's plan. God foresaw it and chose to use it as the means of achieving man's redemption; but he was able to achieve it by Christ's perfect obedience and loyalty to the spirit of love. That obedience and loyalty made him choose deliberately something which he could easily have avoided. And that choice puts the cross into a different category from any mere crime. So God took what otherwise would have been in the same category as other hideous crimes which disfigure history, and made it the means of man's salvation, so that the cross carries God's meaning, not man's. What was, on one side, the work of man's wicked hands was also the work of God's "determinate counsel and foreknowledge." Having thought out the relation between God's foreknowledge and human events, we can see that although God knew the cross must happen, and in co-operation with a loyal Christ used it so gloriously, it was not caused by God's foreknowledge but by man's evil heart. Only Christ's

[5] *His Life and Ours,* pp. 250-51. The Abingdon Press. *Discipleship,* pp. 104 ff. The Abingdon Press.

perfect attitude to the suffering thus thrust upon him enabled God to achieve, through the cross, the salvation of the world.

Perhaps it is not irreverent to put it thus. It is as though God said, "I know that man's misused free will and ignorance and folly will all conspire to bring my beloved Son to the cruel cross, but in that very blackest act of man I will win my victory." In a sense, therefore, God willed the cross, namely, in the sense that he willed and achieved a mighty redemptive act through it; but its circumstances leaped from the sinning heart of man, which we can never equate with the Divine intention.

If war breaks out and a father says to his son, "I want you to join the army and win some tributes of recognition for your bravery," we cannot say that the father willed the war. We cannot say that the father willed that his son should fight. We can say that the father willed the heroic achievement, the circumstances of which were provided by the wickedness of a world. Again and again in history, at the very points of man's greatest defeats, the help of God has meant that his greatest victories have been won.

We may say, in conclusion, that God's ideal intention is health of mind and body and soul, but some of us must pay for the family sins and follies and ignorance. Some of us must help God carry the burden of the world and share in his sufferings. What we can do is to repudiate completely that our sufferings are a personal penalty imposed arbitrarily by a God conceived of as separated from his universe. What we can do, as I hope to show later, is to grasp that suffering, and by our attitude toward it turn it into an asset, our cross of pain into a cross of gold which shines for all to see, kindling faith in a God who takes the pain he did not will, and, so far from being defeated by it, uses it as an instrument, and the willing sufferer as an agent, to fulfill his mighty purposes at last.

CHAPTER VII

WHAT IS GOD'S ATTITUDE TOWARD OUR SUFFERING?

A CLUE which has helped me greatly in the attempt to find my way through the dark forest of human suffering is the thought, borne in upon me, more and more, of the attitude of God to suffering. Does he merely look down upon it from outside it, as I might sit on some stone wall in the course of a country walk and watch ants busily at work on the soil at my feet?

Christian theology teaches both the transcendence and the immanence of God. It is not very easy to hold both in the mind at once. Christian theology has dismissed the idea of pantheism as insufficient. Pantheism teaches that all things are God, that God does not exist apart from the world, and that the world does not exist apart from God. Seeking to make God near and close, it really takes him from us, for he is thought of as an impersonal Force, not as a Person whom we can love. The Christian Church cannot accept the view that God does not exist apart from the world. The world may be thought of as part of his garment, but if the garment were destroyed, God would not perish. Christian theology therefore teaches that God is above the world and outside it and yet, at the same time, within it. He is both transcendent and immanent.

If we can combine the two ideas, they will give us, together, the worthiest conception of God's relation to the universe. We need them both. The idea of transcendence is essential to any conception of the majesty of God. He must not be thought to be imprisoned within his universe. If the universe disappeared altogether, God would still exist. Yet God does not watch the universe as a little boy watches a clockwork train going round and round the lines. In a sense, for which probably we have no adequate means of expression, he is immanent in it.

Illustrations must not be used as though they were arguments, but perhaps some help can be got by thinking of a man in relation to his own hand. He is outside it and in a sense above it. If his hand were amputated, he himself would still exist and manifest his existence in other ways; yet, in a sense, he is immanent in his hand. He directs the work it does. He feels anything that happens to it and his mind consciously or unconsciously controls its muscular movements. Even the circulation of the blood within it is controlled by the unconscious part of the man's mind. It might not be far from the truth to say that God dwells outside the universe in such a way that he is independent of it; but also he controls it, feels all those things which happen to it, and the working of his mind within it is essential, every second, to the continuation of its existence. In him we live and move and have our being and in him all things hold together.[1]

The difficulty is to escape the idea of space. It seems such a necessity to our human thinking. For instance, when we gather in a church to worship, we often thank God for his presence. We think of him as *there,* and so he is, but not in a spatial sense. Just as the little boy in the story could not put his hand over a teacup and sup-

[1] Acts 17. 28. Colossians 1. 17.

pose that because God was everywhere he had "a little bit of him in *there*," so we cannot without inaccuracy of thought clap our hand down even in imagination on a church and think of God as *there,* or on some beautiful island and think of him as *there,* or on a universe and think of him as *there.* The word "there" is a spatial word and God does not dwell in space like a diffused gas.

As a matter of accurate thinking it is not correct to say that God is any*where* because the word "where" is a spatial word, and a spirit does not occupy space. All this may sound pedantic to the reader, but it is essential to think thus in order to see the truth clearly. When we say God is "here" and God is "there," we only do so because it is simpler to do so. In fact, such language is a concession to the human limitations of our thought. It is only correct to say that God is *everywhere available,* and when we say that God dwells within us we mean that he expresses himself through us.

Here is a conception that is going to help us in regard to suffering. A stone can express God, and those of us who have had the privilege of looking at a very thin shaving of granite or marble under a powerful microscope have wondered with awe at the marks of a divine design. But a flower can express him to a greater degree, because it is higher in the scale of being. We find that the higher we go the more completely God expresses himself, and the perfect man was the most complete revelation of God the world has seen, the most complete revelation of God we are capable of apprehending while we remain in the flesh.

To put the point from another angle, we may say that God is most immanent in that which least hinders his expression. Let me repeat, this does not mean there is more of God in this than in that, for there again we are using terms in which God cannot be understood. God is seeking to pour himself through every means of expression; but he is continually hindered because of the incapability of the mediums. I presume that this idea is behind the saying, "God sleeps in the tree, dreams in the animal, wakes in the man." Now, if God's immanence is conditioned by the medium through which he is operating, then whenever there is disharmony in the medium there is injury to God; wherever the medium fails to fulfill its own perfect function, at that point God is prevented from fully expressing his intention and purpose through it. To put the matter very simply, if a child crushes a lily in its hand, then the lily, its beauty supposedly destroyed, becomes incapable of expressing the immanence of God; just as a man's hand, crushed in a machine, becomes thereby incapable of expressing man's purpose, doing what he wants done, and so on. We do not find it hard, then, to understand the inwardness of Christ's reference to a sparrow's fall. God has a purpose even in the life of an individual sparrow. God, in a sense, is immanent in that little bit of his own being, and when it falls to the ground because, perhaps, some boy has thrown a stone at it, then God, in a real sense, is injured, and the measure of the injury is the measure of the incapability of the sparrow further to express the purpose of God. "Not a sparrow falleth to the ground," said Jesus, "without your heavenly Father." For, in a measure already noted, God is hurt—we have no other word—by the fall of the sparrow, by an injury to a medium which was carrying a purpose, a divine intention, and the measure of the injury was the measure of immanence.

Now, if it is true to say that God is injured wherever there is disharmony in a part of the universe which carries his purpose, it is most certainly true to say that God is injured most in that part of the universe which is most expressive of his own being, namely, man. It is the whole argument of Jesus that if what we have seen to be true is true in the case of a sparrow, how much more so is it true in the case of a man? "Ye are of more value," says Jesus, "than many sparrows," not because two sparrows can be sold for a farthing and a man might conceivably fetch twenty-five dollars, but because a man, by comparison, is a much more perfect medium of God's immanence, and expresses God in fuller measure.

We are driven, then, to contemplate a God who carries our sorrows in a sense that is overwhelming and awe-inspiring. It is so tremendous that many have felt that it simply must be rejected. Yet for myself I cannot escape the evidences of its truth. In a sentence it comes to this, that the sufferings of men are the sufferings of God. Indeed, it cannot even be put like that. The sufferings of men are a shadow. The substance is an anguish, poignant and terrible, which only the heart of God could bear. We must hasten to say, at once, of course, that God does not bear physical pain, since he is spirit. Von Hugel[2] has made this point very clear to us in his famous essay. There he uses the word "sympathy." "God cannot suffer," he says, "but he has sympathy with us." Yet I feel that the word "sympathy," as commonly understood, is not nearly eloquent enough. When I sympathize with a person, however deeply, I am outside that person. I may long to get within his very being to *suffer with* him, as the word

[2] *Essays and Addresses*, Second Series, p. 241.

"sympathy" implies. And if the one who suffers is dear to me, my little son, let us suppose, then I would give anything if I could suffer as he does and bear his anguish with him, even if I cannot bear it for him. I would like to become an extension of his body so that I could share the pain that tortures it. But though I take him in my arms and hold him close—an embrace which always seems to me a physical expression of the desire to get even closer, to draw the little suffering personality within one's own personality—yet I remain outside. I suffer, but I am transcendent only—not, accurately speaking, even that. I certainly cannot achieve immanence.

If we are the children of God and are suffering, he not only puts everlasting arms around us and draws us very close; he is also immanent. We are, in a real sense, part of himself, and the suffering, which is ours in terms of pain, is his in terms of something which is much more intimate than sympathy. If I, with a human brain and mind, and human nerves, can suffer a certain amount of anguish because a loved one suffers, what are the sensibilities of an infinite spirit which is only imperfectly manifested through such coarse things as brain and mind and nerves? The fact has got to be faced, even though it seems insupportable and terrible, that the anguish of God, through human suffering, is something which we have no means of measuring and no mind great enough to understand. As I have said in another place, when we petulantly ask of any human tragedy, "Why does God allow this to happen?" we ought to complete the question and ask, "Why does God allow this to happen to himself?"[3]

[3] *Discipleship*, p. 145. The Abingdon Press.

Walt Whitman showed the inwardness of the point I am trying to make when he said, "I do not ask the wounded person how he feels, I myself become the wounded person."[4] One's only criticism of Whitman's line is that I cannot, with all the good will in the world become the wounded person.

The relation of this to sin probably will not need working out, for the reader will realize it. Sin is the greatest disharmony in the universe, greater even than physical suffering, however terrible. God is most deeply wounded at the point where the harmony of his universe is most grievously broken, and we are not surprised to find that the teaching of the New Testament is that our sins are a crucifixion of God. "Sin," cried Joseph Parker, "is a raised hand, and a clenched fist and a blow in the face of God." The sin that crucified Jesus drove its nails not only through the hands of a Man but into the heart of God. I have seen in Italy a picture of the crucifixion, in which, behind the cross, there is a most marvelous portrayal, very faint but unmistakable, of God himself supporting Christ, but wounded with the wounds Christ suffered. And the face of God carries an anguish such as I have never seen portrayed on canvas anywhere else. Just as God bears our sufferings, so he bears our sins. As Saint Paul said, "Him who knew no sin he made to be sin on our behalf." If sometimes we think that it costs us a lot to live in a world like this, where so many terrible things can happen to us, we may at least reflect that it costs God a lot more to make and to sustain a world like this. If the contemplation of the sufferings of another could produce stigmata on the hands of Saint Francis,

[4] *Song of Myself*, Walt Whitman.

so that his hands and feet and side actually showed the marks of the wounds which his mind had pondered so deeply as he knelt before his crucified Lord, what do many things in such a universe as this do with the heart of the Eternal? If Mencius could say in regard to the dikes in China which held back the water, "I feel responsible for every man who drowns in China," what does an infinite and loving God, who is immanent in every life, feel about those who suffer either in mind or body? If a Chinese patient could say of Doctor Hall, "He took my sickness into his own heart,"[5] then are we surprised to hear a prophet crying out, "In all their affliction he was afflicted . . . in his love and in his pity he redeemed them; and he bare them and carried them all the days of old." "He bare the sin of many!" "He was wounded for our transgressions, he was bruised for our iniquities: the chastisement of our peace was upon him: and with his stripes we are healed."[6] I think it is because of this dread thought of the sufferings of God that some learned writers have taught the annihilation of the impenitent. They think that those souls which finally reject God simply cease to exist. Yet perhaps we can see that this is cutting the knot because it is so hard to untie it. "Final ruin," says Bishop Gore, "may involve, I cannot but think, such a dissolution of personality as carries with it the cessation of personal consciousness."[7] But an annihilated soul is a defeat of God, and I think God will not be content with a victory which has necessitated the cessation of the consciousness even of one soul in the universe. Certainly, no

[5] *Christ and Human Suffering,* E. Stanley Jones, p. 158. The Abingdon Press.
[6] Isaiah 63. 9. Isaiah 53. 12 and 5.
[7] *Immortality,* p. 92 ff.

human father would be content with such a solution to a problem. The good shepherd seeketh the lost sheep *until he find it,* and the woman seeks her coin *until she find it.* When we think that the flame of goodness has been extinguished, divine and loving eyes may still see a flickering spark.

> "Beneath the veriest ash there hides a spark of soul
> Which, quickened by love's breath, may yet pervade the whole
> O' the grey, and free again be fire."[8]

I cannot imagine an infinite and omnipotent and loving God sitting down on the throne of the universe in the consummation of his glory when that glory has only reached its consummation by the expedient of driving the souls of some, however few, out into the darkness of annihilation.

But we must not stop there. We need to realize two other very important points about God's attitude toward suffering. The first is the eternal joy of God. Our understanding of God, in this human existence of ours, is, we feel, incomplete and small. We confuse joy with such things as gaiety, mirth, laughter, pleasure, and happiness. The psychologist would come to our aid if we should let him, to show us that joy is not an emotion but a sentiment. By that he means that joy is a deep fount of utter contentment which sometimes springs up into the emotions of gaiety and laughter and so on. But a thing like sorrow or catastrophe which can dry up the surface emotions, cannot touch the deep well of sentiment. The sentiment goes on existing even though the emotions on the surface of the mind may seem, to the casual onlooker, to deny joy

[8] Browning, "Fifine."

Who has not seen a Christian smiling through his tears? Sorrow has ended for the time being the surface emotions of gaiety and laughter, but his joy no man taketh from him. A true idea of Christian joy might more easily be reached by realizing that its opposite is not sorrow. The opposite of Christian joy is unbelief.

Perhaps the point can be made clear by a comparison with other sentiments. Friendship is a sentiment, a deep well, constructed at cost, the construction taking, possibly, a long time. Friendship is a sentiment capable of throwing up all sorts of emotions. But temporary emotions pass. Deeply rooted sentiments remain.

Patriotism is a sentiment, a deep love of country gradually strengthened through the years. It may express itself in surface emotions such as pride in one's country, shame if one's country does something unworthy, even hate if someone treats one's country basely, fear lest the true interests of one's country be attacked, and so on. But whatever happens to the surface emotions the sentiment remains untouched.

Now, in the same way one supposes that there is joy, as a deep and abiding sentiment, in the heart and mind of God. The sentiment of joy in the Christian persists, we say, through all pains and sorrows. Even "though *joys* be withered up and dead," his ultimate belief in God remains unaffected, and joy persists.

Underneath the terrible anguish of God which none can fathom, there is the deep sentiment of joy, because, if one may reverently say it, God believes in himself; he knows his own mind and he knows the end to which the universe is tending. He knows that in spite of all that is grieving him now, and, indeed, that through it, he can ultimately win. The picture of God which one may be allowed reverently to paint on the canvas of one's mind, is that of a face smiling with an ineffable radiance through tears more bitter than human eyes have ever known.

The second point I want to make I have borrowed from Canon Streeter.[9] He calls it the "law of the augmentation of values," and he tells us that he has borrowed it from the Danish philosopher Höffding. In a few sentences the point is this: values in the spiritual world are like energy in the physical world. We are taught the law of the conservation of energy, that though energy may be altered in its manifestation, it cannot be created or destroyed. Canon Streeter's idea is that "whenever any good thing seems to perish, there will appear in its place not an equivalent good but a far better thing." He feels that good in the moral sphere is like energy in the physical; it can never be destroyed but only transformed, so that whatever appears to be lost, inevitably returns in another form. "After tribulation, restoration; after crucifixion, more than a kind of carrying on, a bare niggardly defeat of death and pain, but a resurrection." "The human general," says Canon Streeter, "thinks in terms of companies and battalions; his aim is the victory of the army as a whole. Individual losses, partial and local reverses are just so much sheer loss, regrettable but inevitable, to be written off the total account like bad debts from a tradesman's ledger. But the mind of God has not these anthropomorphic limitations. He thinks not only in terms of battalions but also in terms of individuals, and his victory consists, not merely in the advance of the army as a whole,

[9] Essay on "God and the World's Pain" in *Concerning Prayer*, p. 6. The Macmillan Company, New York.

but also in the power to transform temporary and local losses and reverses into actual gains. Evil is evil and loss is loss, but God has the power, out of, and through the evil and the loss, to bring good and gain, just as the farmer can make the filth of the midden the source of renewed fertility to his land."

A conversation with a Persian student who is studying medicine in this country gave me the chance of confirming some observations I made when I was in Persia. When they are making a Persian rug, they put it up vertically on a frame, and little boys, sitting at various levels, work on the wrong side of it. The artist stands on the right side of the rug, the side on which people will tread, and shouts his instructions to the boys on the other side. Sometimes a boy will make a mistake in the rug. I have a Persian rug in my possession, given me by an Arab sheikh whose guest I was for some time in Mesopotamia. The pattern of the rug suddenly develops a yellow irregularity. Indeed, such asymmetry in design is a mark that a Persian rug was made in Persia and not in Wolverhampton! I said to the student, "What happens when the boy makes a mistake?"

"Well," he said, "quite often the artist does not make the little boy take out the wrong color. If he is a great enough artist, he weaves the mistake into the pattern."

Is there not here a parable of life? You and I are working on the wrong side of the rug. We cannot watch the pattern developing. I know I put in the wrong color very often. I put in black when God meant red, and yellow when he meant white; and the other workers with whom I make my rug make mistakes too. Sometimes I am tempted to say, "Is there Anybody on the other side of the rug; am I just left to make a mess of my life alone? Is there *Anybody* there?" Then, through the insight which comes back with returning faith, I realize that instead of making me undo it all or letting my life's purpose be ruined, God puts more in. I wonder if sometimes he alters the pattern? It isn't what it might have been; but because he is such a great Artist I haven't quite spoiled everything. So, at the end, when he calls me down off my plank and takes me round to the other side, I shall see that just because he is such a great Artist, no mistakes of mine can utterly spoil the pattern; nothing can divert his purpose ultimately, or finally spoil his plan. If only I will work with him, "simply trusting every day," I think one day I shall find my mistakes and my calamities and my distress and my failures and all my pain, woven into the pattern, and I shall say, "It is the Lord's doing, and it is marvelous in our eyes." Some such faith I must have to believe in a God of love who puts us into a world where things can go so utterly wrong.

So, I believe, God can show us the answer to our questions, not by a kind of logic, which, to cover all the ground of the mystery of suffering, would have to be so deep that we could not follow it; but I believe that by faith, hanging on in the dark, going on co-operating with him, putting our life into his hands and not worrying too much as to whether it is not a far greater calamity than he can deal with, he can bring us to the goal of our desires, and the goal of all his purpose.

So often we think the plan of our life has gone wrong or that God has forgotten us. We would not have had life so. Our life's course may take some hidden turn and we may feel that any change in what looked like the original plan is a calamity. But I wonder if, after all, it is only that the roses in our garden are white and we would have had them red.

"My garden has roses red,
 My garden has roses white;
But if when the day is sped
 I stand by the gate at night,
One fragrance comes, when the day is dead,
From my roses white and my roses red.

"The roses of joy are red,
 The roses of pain are white;
But I think, when the day is sped
 And I stand by the gate at night,
I shall know just this, when the day is dead,
That a rose is sweet be it white or red."[10]

[10] "Roses," from *Poems and Sonnets*, Percy Ainsworth.

CHAPTER VIII

MAN'S FIGHT AGAINST SUFFERING

It is admitted that God is responsible for the system on which the world is arranged. He is not responsible for the extent to which that system has got out of gear through the false reactions of men, and though God has made himself responsible for putting it right, he cannot do so—a limitation imposed by himself on himself—without the co-operation of man. Man's attitude toward suffering, therefore, is not to be thought of simply as resignation. If suffering were the will of God in the ordinary sense of the words, then the only pious, and, indeed, logical, thing we could do would be to bow the head without stirring a finger to help ourselves. But if suffering is not the will of God; if God is always on the side of curative and therapeutic agencies, it is man's responsibility to co-operate, as far as he possibly can, so that perfect health, for himself and others, may be reached.

Here again there is a good deal of false thinking. Suffering is sometimes talked about as though through it men were turned into saints. This is far from being the truth. Men become saints not through suffering but through their attitude toward suffering. Rather than say that they have become saints through suffering, it would be truer to say they have become saints in spite of it. Indeed, disease and ill health are enemies of healthy religion. The natural result of suffering is not saintliness, but rebellion, resentment, bitterness, and despair. If anybody imagines that suffering automatically brings saintliness, let him ask himself the question next time he has an abscess at the root of a tooth. If severe abdominal pain comes to him, let him comfort himself by murmuring, "Never mind, every moment I am becoming more and more saintly." And let him make sure that his wife agrees with his conclusion.

When we remember the suffering saints, we need to pay them a great tribute. They have fought a grim battle with illness, which is the natural enemy of religion. They have conquered the temptation to give way to resentment. They have turned, by a marvelous alchemy, the liability into an asset. Suffering has awakened their spirit and called forth from it its highest response, and we cannot praise them too highly.

But supposing the spirit could have been awakened within them in some other way and yet just as completely. Would it not be true to say that their efficiency would have been even greater, for the simple reason that they could have offered to God, then, a more perfect instrument for his purposes? It is incredible to suppose that Jesus would have been more holy if he had been a dyspeptic or lame. If the spirit is fully awakened, as fully awakened as any illness or suffering could awaken it, then surely it is God's highest purpose that the physical instrument which we wish to put into his hand should be as free from limitations as possible. We may even say that maximum spiritual efficiency *in a fully awakened person,* is not reached apart from maximum physical efficiency, except in such cases in which suffering is voluntarily accepted for an heroic purpose. For the general run of men, spiritually awakened and eager to dedicate themselves to God as completely as they can, it is true to say that they cannot be as good as they might be unless they are as fit as they can be. It is impossible to suppose that Christ removed an essential aid to spiritual development when he healed men of their physical sufferings. The asceticism of the monks was probably an aid to physical fitness. I cannot but believe that their self-flagellation was definitely outside the purposes of God. Most of us realize a sense of the presence of God far more keenly when our physical powers are at their height than, shall we say, when we are slowly recovering from a severe attack of influenza. Suffering does not, of itself, bring gain to character.

Our first point, then, would seem to be this: that so far as in us lies it is a spiritual duty to fight and, if possible, overcome disease. Although God has a very tender word for all those who are laid aside by suffering, it is his ideal intention that all should be fit and well—save in those cases where men and women deliberately court suffering for some high goal which otherwise could not be reached—and that merely to throw up our hands and resign ourselves to pain, without using all the resources which are in our power, would be to give up any serious attempt to do the will of God. One of the greatest tragedies in the world is the fact that a number of people are ill who might be well if all the resources of the human family were used to bring them health. Through the slow pace of the family progress their capability of being used in the hands of God is, to some extent, lowered.

Man's attitude toward pain must be, therefore, in the first place, to fight it with all the means at his disposal. As our ancestors fought the wild beasts and drove them back from their villages, and, in this country, exterminated those which were most dangerous, so it seems to be the plan of God that we shall fight and overcome the ravages of the germs of disease, combat all bad conditions which bring disease to man and menace his happiness, and make tireless war against every agency which is capable of bringing the terrible sufferings which we see around us. Man is to be master of all created things, whatever the beneficent intention of their creation may be in certain directions, and he is to prevent them from injuring his own health.

In this great battle man must use every weapon he can. Naturally, in a case of physical suffering, he will, if he is wise, call in medical and, if need be, surgical aid. Through the brains and fingers of this great profession there is not just the skill and knowledge which the individual doctor has obtained, but in that doctor's training there is gathered together all that is valuable in the whole of medical and surgical science since the days of Hippocrates. If medical and surgical aid are not those most fitted to bring relief, then the patient must turn to other methods through which the power of God flows and the purposes of God are achieved. It is probable that psychological methods will increasingly be shown to be useful in dealing with certain cases of suffering, not only mental but physical, for again and again, as I have tried to show elsewhere, even physical suffering is often a translation, into the physical realm, of a conflict which exists in the mind, especially when that conflict functions so deep in the mind that the sufferer is not conscious of it. I am quite certain that a good deal, even of what is called organic disease, is only the physical symptom of a much deeper disharmony which exists in the mind or the soul of the sufferer, and the co-operation of psychological investigation, with the assurance which great religious truths bring to the mind, suggests and opens up an avenue for helping sufferers which will more and more be explored and used.[1]

If I were suffering physically, I think I should not despise any method through which the healing and renewal, which I believe God intends should come to men and women, might be brought to my aid.

I have devoted a chapter to the weapons of faith and prayer in man's fight against suffering.

Just as we must investigate the way in which medical, surgical, and psychological methods can best be made operative and potent for sufferers, so we must work at the ways in which faith can be called out and prayer made potent to heal. Prayer, of course, is always to be used, whether it brings relief from suffering or not. It does bring strength and a quiet mind. Jesus prayed in the Garden that the cup might pass from him, and it did not pass, yet the prayer was not unanswered. It brought him the assurance that he was in the hands of God and that everything he suffered would be used. And the intention of the prayer was answered, that he might perfectly do God's will.

One of the things prayer does in the battle against suffering is to alter the effect of suffering on the patient's mind and heart. It prevents the resentment and despair of which we have spoken, and it supports the patient's spirit and hope and optimism. A Harley Street specialist once said, in my presence, that again and again, in his experience, the visit of a minister who knew his job had made just the difference to the mentality of the patient which

---

[1] This idea is worked out more fully in *Psychology and Life*. The Abingdon Press.

tipped the swinging balance down on the side of recovery. We are to use prayer as a powerful ally whatever other agencies are employed. As Sir Oliver Lodge once remarked, "It is not really absurd to suggest that drugs and no prayer may be about as foolish as prayer and no drugs."

I know, of course, that prayer must not be thought of simply as a form of treatment, a kind of spiritual plaster which is worth trying because it may heal and, at any rate, will allay psychological irritation. It is the loftiest activity of the spirit, and its true goal is the glory of God. But God will not despise us if, in our agony, we cannot think thus, but can only cry to him to help us. And by prayer we are putting ourselves in touch with Infinite Life and Power and Love and with the Central Calm of the Universe, and that is the privilege of the sons and daughters of God.

In speaking of man's attitude toward suffering we must include suffering which is voluntarily accepted for some great purpose. Here the problem is entirely different. Man's attitude, then, is that he has definitely undertaken suffering because it is going to bring a higher good to others. In other words, the measure of good which is to be reached through suffering is more than worth the suffering involved. We think at once of a man like Oates, realizing that his frost-bitten feet are holding up progress, going out into the snow to lay down his life. We think of a man like Father Damien deliberately going to a leper settlement, where contracting the disease was practically a certainty, that he might minister to others. And we think most of all of Christ, setting his face like a flint to go to Jerusalem, knowing what it would mean for him, and yet, for our sakes, never hesitating, never faltering, never looking back. Such illustrations as these make us bow down in humble gratitude and admiration. There is no problem here to be discussed. We can only rejoice.

Now let us consider what is to be man's attitude toward suffering in those cases where the suffering is incurable. Let us imagine a man who has been able to use all the agencies known to humanity in the fight against pain. He has had first-class opinions from all those whose lives are dedicated to relieving the distresses of minds and bodies. He has used, as powerfully as he knows how, the agencies of faith and prayer, and still his suffering remains. What is he to do next?

Here one treads with reverent steps, but one does feel justified in saying that "resignation" is not the word to describe what his attitude should be. "Rebellion" is certainly not the word. The finest attitude is acceptance and glad co-operation; as though a man is really saying: "I still don't think that it is God's will that I should suffer thus, but the agencies at my disposal have not met with success. In other words, God's perfect will cannot yet be done because of human ignorance or some kind of human hindrance somewhere. Therefore I must accept this suffering. God's will, *under these conditions,* is that I should offer my suffering to him and to co-operate with him so that, out of this suffering, a glorious purpose may be achieved." He can take this attitude while he still goes on trying new methods and using new weapons in his battle against suffering. Though many, in doing this, have not successfully fought their own pain, their tireless battle has opened up methods which others have taken up, modified and extended and used successfully. Further, most sufferers could truly say that, even though they are laid aside, they can still count for much in the world spiritually, for they have time to pray and meditate and think, which they never took when health was theirs. I stated earlier that if the human spirit is fully awakened and is responding fully to God, then the maximum spiritual efficiency is reached by putting a perfect physical instrument into God's hands; but how many of us in full health are thus responding? For myself I know how many sufferers put my life to shame. From their couches of pain they exert a far greater spiritual power than I, in my busy life, exert. Suffering, when joyously accepted, certainly carries the sufferer much further than most people go who have perfect health. The sufferer then may feel that what he is bearing is his share of the world's burden, the burden of ignorance and folly and sin; and he may truly feel that he is sharing this in partnership with God, whom we have seen to be the Bearer of so heavy a burden.

Perhaps it may not be said too often that we live in a world so constituted that ten thousand things can happen to us which are not the will of God, but nothing can happen to us which cannot be captured for God. In a world where free will enters in so greatly and in which man learns slowly and through many mistakes; in a world where the individual suffers through the crisscross of other people's follies and other people's sins, it is impossible to hold that all that comes to the individual is the intention of God. The glorious truth, however, is that nothing can possibly happen to us but that, by taking the right attitude toward it, we can win from it a valuable spiritual asset instead of letting it lie as a depressing liability.

When the Nile overflowed and "spread its obliterating deposit of black mud over the field hardly won from the desert and watered at such cost of patient toil, the victor over it was not the engineer stemming its current with his barricade, but the inspired peasant who, greatly daring, flung his precious rice into its forbidding ooze."[2] One of the meanings of omnipotence is that nothing can happen to us which has any inherent power to smash us. Nothing can happen to us from which we cannot gather a harvest.

There is a secret running through the New Testament, a secret which Jesus possessed and taught, and it is worth turning aside to watch that secret unfolding in his life from early days until, at last, he was so truly the master of it that he could apply it to his sufferings and use it to become the Master of his cross. We shall have to *learn* it. And we shall only learn it by doing what he did. He applied it to the little things of life first. He learned by the things he suffered,[3] and he went on to capture for God the greatest suffering in the world.

The old alchemists dreamed of and sought to find a substance which, as soon as it touched other substances, would turn them into gold. They never found it. But in the moral sphere Jesus found it. It was a certain kind of reaction to experience. It was a certain kind of attitude toward life. We know how the analytical chemist can mix two colorless liquids together and a precipitate is formed in his test tube. Then he adds the right reagent and the precipitate disappears. It is dissolved. The very nature of the substance in the tube is altered by the addition of the right reagent.

Jesus always knew the right reagent to use so that the nature of a happening could be changed to spiritual advan-

---

[2] *Grace and Personality*, p. 10, Oman.
[3] See Hebrews 5. 8.

tage. He did not believe that everything that happened to him was the will of God rigidly worked out. He knew that many things happen which are not the will of God. They may be due to mistakes or ignorances; in our case, sins. They may be due to those of other people. But nothing could happen to him which he could not use for God's glory.

Jesus took the dull metal of life's commonplace circumstances, life's monotonies, life's trivialities, life's accidents, and by his attitude toward them he changed them into shining gold. Thus he showed what true religion is. Religion is not purely a matter of understanding and believing certain theological and metaphysical doctrines or creeds. It is not a certain mystical experience which only emotional natures can ever really have in any full sense—a misconception which has caused much secret wonderment to certain magnificent souls, some of whom have even tried to be sentimental in the hope of getting what so many regard as the only valid sign of a religious life. Religion is a right attitude. It is a right attitude toward God, toward one's neighbor, and toward *life.*

We will consider here the right attitude toward life, because that is what we mean by the alchemy of Jesus: the power to change the result of a happening and make it redound to the glory of God and the spiritual gain of the person concerned. That which would cause most folk to worry themselves to death, Jesus made the secret beginning of a new trust in God. That which would cause us to sweat with fear, became to him the spring of a deeper courage. That temptation which would overwhelm most men and bring their lives down in shame and ruin, became to him the iron which entered into his character and made it stronger than ever. That suffering which would make most men lose all faith in a loving, omnipotent God, became in his hands, and through his attitude toward it, the inspiration of the whole of Christendom ever since. In every Christian church in the world men gather in spirit around his cross. Circumstances which to most of us would mean defeat, depression, despair, or at least a fatalistic bowing to the supposed will of God, became to him a challenge which he gladly took us, always to emerge more than conqueror. He literally was, and will show us how to be, more than conqueror. It was not as if the difficulty were just neutralized. Its nature, purpose, and tendency were reversed. The amount which would have to be, for most men, entered into the devil's credit account, he did not merely wipe off. It was entered into the credit account of God, with no liability up against it. Liabilities became assets.

Jesus began with little things in his home. Look at him there, where again and again there must have been happenings which tend to jar and fret a sensitive spirit. We must consider what sort of a home it was. We know it was a poor home, not only because Jesus was a carpenter, but from the fact that whenever, in his subsequent ministry, he led men's minds from the dear familiar things of earth, to the sublime things of heaven, he never spoke as the son of a rich man would have spoken. In his stories the candle lights the whole house; only a one-roomed house then. Jesus seems to have memories of garments patched and repatched. When he speaks of food, it is of fish and bread, the food of the very poor. This is not a home in which plenty of money makes for smooth working. Moreover, Mary was not always that sweet and gentle and understanding person she is sometimes represented to have been. She lets it be known publicly that she thinks Jesus is mad. There is a world of pathos in his word that all who do his will are his true relatives. Those who are misunderstood at home have a great friend in Jesus, who has passed that way before them.

Again, very early, Jesus became the breadwinner. His father died when he was little more than a boy. He had five brothers and two sisters. Were they never noisy, troublesome, sick?

> "What was he doing all that time,
> From twelve years old to manly prime?
> Was he, then, idle, or the less
> About His Father's business?"

No! As the days passed he was conscious of a light growing brighter and brighter, like some gradual and splendid dawn. He knew that he was near to the Father in a sense no one else either experienced or understood. He growingly realized that God wanted him for some mighty work. Yet the little cottage could still hold him. The household tasks did not fret him. The noisy children never angered him. He was meeting all these little happenings with his secret alchemy. He was turning them all into gold. He knew that they could all be made to fit in somehow. He knew that all things work together for good to those who love God enough to trust him. The parables which have thrilled the world were preceded by a training in telling stories to children when he took them off his mother's hands to give her an hour of peace. So the problems of a little home and a big family became the preparation for God's wider purposes.

See him in business. He has nine mouths to fill. That means working hard, early and late. There were no trade unions then. All the time there is growing the conception of what he has come into the world to do. Moreover, were customers never tiresome, never exasperating? Did the nails never slip from his fingers? Was the plane always sharp for him? Was the wood never knotted and tough? Yet in the early life of Jesus there is no suspicion of complaining, of chafing, of unrest. He does not rebel against the smallness of his sphere. He loves God and goes on, knowing that it will all be worked into God's plan if he himself takes the right attitude toward life. And when he had done twenty years in a carpenter's shop, before he had preached a single sermon, his Father said, "This is my beloved Son, in whom I am well pleased." He has a secret. He is preparing for his cross.

So it is with everything that happens to him. Bereavement itself, which, for so many, is life's greatest mystery, does not leave him untouched. His cousin, John Baptist, whom he loved, and who seemed to understand him better than most, is beheaded to please the whim of a nautch girl. What did some of us say—perhaps about the Kaiser—when our loved ones were overtaken by a violent death? With Jesus there is no wild raving against Herod. There is no vehemence about the apparent callousness of God. There is no emphasis on the mystery of death. There is no rebellion. Only this: "Let us go into the desert and rest a while." He will be quiet, and think, and pray. He will take a little time to see what can be made of this happening. He will see the best way to turn it into gold. He has a secret. He is preparing for his cross.

A little later death comes to him. Just as things are

"going," just as the disciples are beginning to understand, just as the ideas which are changing the world are spreading in men's hearts, there looms up the awful shadow of the cross, which a pagan writer calls "that most terrible of all punishments." He was so young to die. It seemed such an anticlimax. It looked like defeat, disaster, the end. Yet in a garden where tears and blood mingled on an anguished face he knew that he must take the same great attitude toward life. He must do the right thing, and he could trust God to see to results. The cross may be the will of Judas and a handful of plotters rather than the will of God, but nothing happens that cannot be captured for God. And this capture was destined for the redemption of the world. That is why the cross is not the wooden, blood-stained, splintered thing it once was. Jesus turned it into gold by his own secret alchemy. It blazes on graves and spires and altars. It is the holiest thing in the world. Its meaning now is triumph, not defeat. His secret saved the world. He was ready for his cross.

Nothing can ever defeat us if we apply to it the alchemy of Jesus. That is his secret of life. But it is an open secret. And if we will come, and listen, and look, he will tell it to us.

Fight your pain, my brother! Use every weapon open to you! But if you deliberately incur suffering because it is a nobler way than to seek escape; or if you cannot yet be healed, accept it in a co-operation with God which can even contain joy, and by that secret alchemy of Jesus make *your* pain also redemptive; and you also will be among those who hold the world in thrall.

CHAPTER IX

THE WEAPON OF PRAYER

ALL of us at some time or another, when we have been in anguish of mind or body, or, even more poignantly, when we have been distressed at the pain of another, have sent out into the ether a passionate prayer for relief and help. Then perhaps there has come upon us the paralyzing doubt that it may make no difference; that the universe is run, down to the tiniest detail, in obedience to inscrutable and immutable laws; and that our little prayers are like the fret of rippling summer waves against a cliff of granite.

Into the dark night of our despair, like a ray of silver light, has come the promise of Jesus, "If ye shall ask anything of the Father, he will give it you in my name."[1] Yet, even then, we have found that the words, however beautiful, seemed untrue for us, for we have asked many things in his name and they have not been granted to us —or is it that we do not know the whole significance of the phrase, "In his name"?

I have before me, as I write, a letter full of faith and trust which I should like to share with the reader. I cannot answer it. Indeed, it needs no answer. Its sublime faith soars above my groveling arguments. It is one of the most beautiful letters I have ever received, and I have the writer's permission to quote it:

"May I tell you a little about what has happened? I do hope it won't bore you, but there is just one thing

[1] John 16. 23.

that does puzzle me. Last April my young sister G. went to Jesus, after two years of awful suffering and agonizing pain. I loved her, ah! so dearly, I don't think I could make you understand just how deeply I cared for her. She was three years my junior when she died, just twenty. We weren't only sisters, we were pals. She was in the hospital on and off for over a year before she died, six months the last time; and, of course, she died there. She faced terrible operations with amazing courage; the doctors and nurses grew to love her because of her high spirits and patience. We wrote to each other daily, until, at last, she was too ill to write and in every letter she would say, 'Do please pray for me, won't you, and ask God to make me well and strong again, and let me come home to you all, because I know if we keep faith in him, he won't fail us; he will make me better.' She did so want to live, but life is very sweet at twenty, isn't it? And she had everything to live for; she had a boy who loved her dearly, and then there was so much she wanted to do for Jesus, whom she served with all the fervor of her young heart. She had great ambitions to be a missionary in West Africa; she had met that great heart, Rev. Harry Webster, and he inspired her with a very great love for that country.

"Almost every hour of every day while she was ill I prayed and asked God to make her better and well and strong again, because in the Bible it says, 'If ye shall ask anything in my name, I will do it.' Now, this is what puzzles me. I did ask him, and I did believe, and I know that G. did, and yet she died. I used to say, 'Oh, dear Jesus, I *know* you are able to do all things, I know you gave back health to broken bodies when you were on earth, please, please bless my darling, and make her well and strong again.' But it failed. I have thought about it such a lot, and I can't understand why it should say, 'If ye shall ask anything in my name, I will do it,' when it doesn't apply to everyone. Can you explain it? Please don't think I have lost faith in God, I haven't; I believe just as firmly as ever I did; I thank him that I have faith to believe where I cannot see. It was G. who showed me the way to Jesus, not by anything particular that she said, but how she lived. Even her suffering and agony, clothed in so wonderful a garment of praise and beauty, brought us closer together in his love.

"Just a month after G. died, Daddy had a stroke, which absolutely paralyzed him down the left side, and after six weeks of great weariness, he died, his heart well-nigh broken. He was the dearest and best father in all the world, and God only knows how much we wanted him to get better, and yet I didn't ask him to make him well again. I knew it was no use; I just asked him to help us to do his will, however hard, and be brave about it. What hurt us all so much about G's. illness, was that she had been such a lovely, bonny, healthy girl, brimming over with life and laughter, and it seemed so awful to see her, week after week, getting worse and worse, despite the skill of clever surgeons and physicians.

"Mummy died when I was fourteen; she was accidentally burned to death, and I remember then I was looking through the Bible, and I came across a verse which said, 'The prayer of faith shall save the sick,' and it seemed such a comfort to me, and so every night and morning I prayed that she would get better. I was quite certain that I had plenty of faith. But she died after six weeks of almost torture. If you have ever come into contact with a serious burning case, you will know what terrible suffering it entails. That was a shock to my childish faith, because I felt *sure* God would make her better, she was so lovely, she seemed to me to be the ideal of motherhood, so patient and loving.

"So you see, I have had rather a lot to shake my faith, haven't I? But my great joy is this, that I still believe that God is love, and that he is my Saviour, more than ever before, and I shall do, please God, whatever happens, because I don't think anything can ever hurt me more than losing G. has done.

"What does puzzle me, as I have said before, is why Jesus should have said what he did, 'If ye shall ask anything in my name, I will do it.' Perhaps it has been a problem to many right down the ages. I don't know; I do know that Jesus wouldn't have said 'anything' unless he meant it, and yet why is it that none of these prayers of mine were answered?

"I know, of course, that it isn't for me to question the authority of Jesus; perhaps I wasn't worthy to ask. I know I have plenty of weaknesses and failings. I am conscious of them all. I know I need the redeeming love of Jesus all the time, to keep me pure and sweet, as he would have me be. . . ."

We have argued in this book that the will of God for everyone is perfect health and strength of body and mind and spirit. How difficult it is, then, for my correspondent, and for thousands like her, to maintain faith in the power of prayer! One has sympathy with those fine souls who gradually drop their belief in prayer and feel that it is a farce. What did Jesus mean by the promise we have quoted?

Although it may sound a weak kind of exegesis, and although one is conscious of the great danger of this kind of argument, I think we are bound to admit, quite honestly, that this saying of Jesus, if accurately reported, is one of those Eastern sayings which, to a Western mind, sounds an exaggeration, but which, to an Eastern mind, is a poetical way of expressing a great truth. The East does not hold the meticulous idea of exactitude which the West demands. The lack of such exactitude in the West is frowned upon and called inaccuracy or something worse, and a speaker who indulged in it would lose a certain authority if—like the late Sadhu Sandar Singh, for example—he related an experience in two different ways to two different audiences; ways which did not strictly agree in detail. The East has never been so enslaved by literal accuracy. If I describe a means of expression as "exaggerated," it is looked upon in the West as a flaw. But in the East it would not be so. Exaggerated language is there used much as we might use a metaphor or other figure of speech, the more forcibly to express an idea. When Jesus says that, "If we have faith, we shall be able to remove mountains into the sea," we do not take it literally. When he says that God cares for us so much that "the hairs of our head are all numbered," we do not take that literally either. In the same way we cannot possibly take it literally when it is promised that *anything* which we are capable of asking in the name of Jesus will be given to us; because man is capable of making absurd requests, requests the granting of which would finally be hurtful to him.

I think that we are to understand that Jesus is trying to paint a picture of a God who is far more eager to give than we are to receive, who is not niggardly and reluctant but who longs to pour all manner of blessings into our lives, but that we, through lack of co-operation with him, do not lay ourselves open to receive them.

No doubt emphasis must be put on the phrase, "In my name." We must not take the space here to argue the point, but, again and again, through the New Testament "name" and "power" are synonymous. Men who went through the known world in the name of Jesus, went in the power of Jesus. What we are asking in our prayers we are asking through the power of Jesus Christ, so that the passage would come to read, "If ye shall ask anything that is in my power to give you, you shall have it." Our discussion of what power is and what it can and cannot achieve is relevant at this point. (See pp. 26ff.)

Constantly we are told to pray, "in the name of Jesus Christ our Lord," or "through Jesus Christ our Lord," and I have gathered the impression that what is meant, beyond the meaning just indicated, is, if the metaphor may be allowed, that all our own desires are to be passed through the mesh of his desire for us, and that anything that is hostile to his mind must be strained out, and only that allowed to go through which is his will for us, as well as our own desire. Then in very truth the passage has abundant fulfillment, for we are only asking what it is God's will to give us.

If you then reply, "Well, what is the need to ask if he wills to give?" I think the answer is that there are many things we cannot receive until we prove ourselves ready to receive them. A sufferer from typhoid fever may pray his relatives for food, but if they are wise they will not answer the prayer in that form until his convalescence has reached a point when food can be beneficially received. Again and again, I think, even in our prayers for deliverance from temptation, we are left to flounder because we will not realize that the power which comes to us can only come from God and from our conscious co-operation with him. God often does not answer either "Yes" or "No." He often says "Wait," and our prayer for deliverance from pain and suffering has to have the answer "Wait," because God wills to answer it through the human family to which we inextricably belong,[2] and the members of that family simply don't know enough to deliver us.

Here we strike again a point already made: that it is God's way of dealing with certain cases of suffering to allow the individual to continue in pain until the human family rouses itself and uses its resources to remove the cause of disharmony. If God immediately answered the prayer of the individual for relief, he would, by that very act, discourage the family from undertaking the research which is educative and which helps it to prevent such suffering and to cure it in the future. He would do for the family what the family *could* do for itself if it used its resources. Here then, for instance, is one of the things which Jesus has no power to do; for he never acts contrary to the will of his Father. "The Son can do nothing of himself, but what he seeth the Father doing,"[3] and he will not answer a prayer of ours if it militates against God's wise plan for his family. In our best moments we do not ask this. We should despise a schoolmaster who granted concessions to an individual child in the school who happened to be his own. It is natural we should *ask*

---

[2] See pp. 77f.
[3] John 5. 10.

for relief from suffering, and God must long for us to have that relief, but we are called upon sometimes to share his burden and suffering while we wait for the greater good of the family to discover its own resources.

One of the thoughts which have paralyzed prayer and made people feel that it cannot be answered is the apparent reign of law. But we must never push our observation of law-abiding energies, and our idolatry of "science," so far as to make us suppose that God has made a certain number of laws of the universe and that now he himself is bound by them, almost in the same way in which a man driving a motor car is limited by what the car can do, and cannot, for example, suddenly soar into the air. People sometimes imagine that God has made the universe, and has, as it were, set it going with a number of laws on board, rather in the same way that a little boy might wind up a clockwork train and set it going, and be unable further to control what happens. I think it is true to say that God never acts in a way which ruptures law, but the influence of laws, one upon the other, can bring about any result which God desires. If certain things do not happen as we should wish them to happen, it is not the iron rule of law which is the factor, but the holy and loving purposes of God.

It is a law that water always runs downhill; but the very fall of water downhill can drive a pump to push water uphill. Law would suggest that iron does not float; but a Cunard liner while at no point bringing about a rupture of law, carries hundreds of tons of iron across the sea. Frequently we are depressed at the thought that whatever a man soweth that shall he also reap; but the teaching of the parable of the sower seems rather conclusively to show that a farmer's troubles are caused because he does not reap what he sows. The birds of the air devour some of it; some of it falls by the wayside and is choked by thorns. We must not think of a God who makes a world so incomplete that, afterward, having established its system of laws, he cannot move to save his children because his own laws defeat him. In a wonderful phrase of Professor Cairns, "The universe is not a steel gauntlet hard and inflexible. It is a silken glove." And what is more wonderful still, it is a silken glove with the hand of God inside it.

We are therefore to pray, and to pray in faith; but as in the case of faith, we are not to test our prayer and call it useless if it does not bring exactly the kind of reply we desire. The chilling thought that God does not answer prayer, that there is a great silence, must be fought off at all costs. There cannot be such a thing as unanswered prayer. How can there be? If God is anything like the God Jesus believed in, a God who is interested in the small details of our lives and knows the sparrow's fall, how can he possibly refrain from any answer at all when his own children, made in his likeness, cry to him? "God is a father," said Jesus. "When ye pray say, Our Father." What sort of a father is he who, when his child cries out to him, averts his face, maintains a stony silence and looks the other way?

At one of the Round Table Conferences which E. Stanley Jones held in India, there was a fine young Englishman, the leader among a group of business men, who wanted better relationships between India and Great Britain. "God let me down," said this young Englishman. "My brother was wounded in the War. I prayed to him that my brother might live. Any decent person would have answered. He did not. My brother died. I have no faith left."

Do we not see here an illustration of the point that there are some circumstances in which God cannot do what we ask? The answer of the individual prayer might let go the greater good of the family. Or, under some circumstances, the misuse of free will and the results of man's folly and sin and ignorance, create a situation to repair which God requires time. To deflect a bullet in answer to a prayer would make religion an insurance and prayer a bribe. To prevent the bullet from pounding through the brain of our loved one because we happen to pray for him, would involve a rearrangement of the whole universe on a plan less good than the present. God's way seems to be to allow evil and folly and ignorance to bring about certain results which offer an endless challenge to the rest of the family, but not to leave the matter there; to act subsequently, indeed, in ways which weave the tragedy into his ultimate plan.

Whenever he can do so, having regard to the family interest, God does answer our prayers in the way we want them answered, and it is evident that, again and again, in cases of suffering, he is able to do things through prayer which are impossible without it.[4] If my loved one were suffering, I should always feel that I must pray. I should not think my prayer was directed toward persuading a reluctant God to intervene, or telling him something he does not know, or getting him to do something which otherwise he would not do. I should regard my prayer as a co-operation with his spiritual laws, similar to the co-operation on the physical level which the doctor

[4] See *Discipleship*, pp. 57ff. The Abingdon Press.

or the surgeon employs, with the additional richness about it that my co-operation brought me into a conscious, personal relationship with him. That point of our cooperation with God through prayer needs to be stressed, for, again and again, in my experience, the prayers of a congregation have so acted upon the mind of a patient, bringing sometimes, but not necessarily, the expectation of recovery, that therapeutic agencies already employed have a far more potent effect, and the mind, which is so powerful an agent on the body, believes in recovery and brings it about.

But the value of prayer in suffering is not fully realized by healing and is not discounted by failure to heal. Its value is seen in the rich fellowship which the sufferer has with God through it. That fellowship can become so wonderful that the patient, while still greatly desirous of being cured, does not feel that there is a mystery left, and, far from any feelings of resentment and rebellion, is able to co-operate with God so that whatever happens the eyes are lifted to the glory of God and the final consummation of his purposes. While I was writing these words I received a letter from an old saint who had enjoyed perfect health until he was seventy-nine. Then he broke a thigh and lay in great pain. "But," he writes, "I never, in all the years of good health, knew such heights of intimate communion with God as I have had since my accident. I feel so grateful."

Saint Paul himself had a thorn in the flesh, which may have been recurrent malaria, or may have been the lameness which hindered him in his long missionary journeys. Whatever it was, he prayed to the Lord "thrice" (the Greek phrase means "repeatedly"). There was an answer, but not the answer he wanted. The reply seems to have been that although the thorn was not the will of God but a "messenger of Satan,"[5] God, for reasons not disclosed to Paul, must not remove it, and Paul was holding on in the faith that God's grace was sufficient for him and that God's strength was made perfect in weakness. But look at Paul's magnificent reply. The relationship between himself and God is so close and rich that he writes, "Most gladly therefore will I rather glory in my weakness that the power of Christ may rest upon me." Paul does not stop praying. He does not "finish with religion." He does not even say, "Isn't it terrible?" not even "It's too bad," or, "I can't think what I've done to deserve it." Although what he desires is not done, the mystery ceases to trouble him and his eyes are lifted to a far horizon.

So it was with Jesus. "If it be possible," he said, "let this cup pass."[6] I am so glad that Jesus said that; that he allows us to breathe our wondering doubts, for had he himself not said, "All things are possible to him that believeth"?[7] Yet he himself shares our doubt, breathes the natural prayer to escape pain and suffering. "If it be possible, let this cup pass."[8] It did not pass. It had to be drunk to the bitter dregs. God cannot do all things, because he must not do all things. And who would say that the great prayer was unanswered? Moreover, Jesus did not "finish with religion." He said, "Nevertheless not what I will, but what thou wilt," believing that God would ultimately reach his goal with yet more glory to

[5] 2 Corinthians 12. 7.
[6] Matthew 26. 39.
[7] Mark 9. 23.
[8] Matthew 26. 39.

his name, and, indeed, with yet more glory to the work of Jesus if the cross were endured.

A little laddie in my own Sunday school, who had been told not to go near an iron grating in the street where he lived, since the grating was known to be loose, disobeyed his mother's instructions, played on the grating, fell through and broke his leg.

Things went wrong, and for a time it was thought that he would never be able to walk again, and, very unfortunately, the nurse was careless enough to let the little chap hear this report. When his mother came to see him she bent over him lovingly and the tears welled up in his big brown eyes. He wound his arms around her neck and said: "Mummy, I know it was my fault and I disobeyed you. But if I can never walk or run again, will you go on loving me?" You can imagine the answer. "Then," said the little chap, smiling through his tears, "I can bear anything."

I must add, though it is irrelevant to our purpose, the joyous ending. I was able to bring, both to the mother and to the boy, news from a great surgeon who is himself a member of my congregation, that the laddie would walk again, and now he is well and strong and running about. But that little chap taught me a lesson. We ask of God a great many things, and some of them cannot be answered. Yet the richest thing in the world is an experience of his love open to us all. If we are quite sure that he goes on loving us, we can bear anything, and even pain can become a sacrament.

CHAPTER X

THE WEAPON OF FAITH

WE are not in much doubt that faith would be a marvelous weapon in the fight against suffering if only we knew what it really is and how to get it. Most of us have seen miracles happen because, it is said, people have had faith. But the contemplation of those miracles has often left us cold. It has left us rather wistful and perhaps a little sad. They seem very lucky people, these people who find it so easy to "have faith." How does one have faith?

Jesus put a great emphasis on it. He rebuked men because they had such little faith. In his picturesque Eastern way he told them that if they only had faith as a grain of mustard-seed, they could move mountains, and apparently his own mighty works depended on their faith.

Saint Paul is not behind his Master in his emphasis on faith. We are to be saved "through faith." We are justified "by faith." The author of the Epistle to the Hebrews puts faith in a place of prime importance for the Christian. And Saint James knew and commended the faith through which men could be healed.

Modern preachers still urge us to trust more in God, and modern healing missions are said to depend for their success on the "faith" of the patients.

It would certainly seem, then, a question of the very greatest importance to ask what faith is, and how, in these modern and scientific days, we may be expected to get it. Merely to say to a person "Have faith," as though one could thereupon proceed to have it, is asking rather more of human nature than it can give. If we could catch a glimpse of the Master; if we could spend an hour with that greatest, that dauntless, heroic apostle of his, then we might make a leap of faith; but living, say, in the drab respectability of a conventional little town, with noisy cars clattering by, it is not easy, at the word of a preacher, to "have faith" in the Man of Galilee. The scientific training most of us have had seems to get in the way of "simple faith."

I want the reader to have a picture in his mind. At the top of an isolated, rocky islet, standing alone in a tempest-tossed sea, is a most beautiful garden. The cliffs, which form the jungly coastline of the mainland, are very near to it. But let us imagine that the chasm between is such that it is impossible to scramble down the shore cliffs, across the space at the bottom and climb the isolated crag. Let us imagine that no bridge is possible and that the only way to get to that garden of desire is to take a run on the mainland and make an adventurous leap. For such a leap the edge is most important. It must be firm and sharp. It must not slope down or crumble. The garden of desire can be reached in no other way but by making a long run along one of the roads leading to the cliff edge and, making use of a good "take-off," leaping high in the air. Then let us imagine that several roads lead toward this chasm, but some are rough and stony and covered with boulders. They haven't been used for a long time. It would be difficult to get the requisite run along them. They have fallen into disrepair, some of them do not run very near the isolated cliff, and the place from which one would want to "take-off" crumbles under one's feet. Yet there is one road, cleared and repaired, every inch of it tested, along which one could run easily and swiftly, and the end is firm and strong. This gives the best chance of a successful leap.

If I have not wasted the last page or so, it will be realized that the leap is the leap of faith which lands us in the place where the soul is content, where the mind can rest. The leap is necessary. That place where the soul rests—we will not be exact about it yet, or call it health, or even salvation—cannot be reached without faith. There must be the leap, with risk and uncertainty. Roads which are largely disused, and have fallen into disrepair, are credulity, for instance, and superstition. By credulity I mean the mind's ability to accept ideas without adequate evidence. By superstition I mean irrational fear of the unknown. The best road is the road of science. I do not, of course, mean science in the narrow sense. When one uses the word "science" one finds that some folk interpret the word to mean only the physical sciences—chemistry and astronomy and physics, for instance. We must remember that theology and psychology are sciences too.

Perhaps a better phrase would be the road of knowing, where knowledge has been tested, tried, and proved. The leap of faith, I hold, is best made by proceeding down that road which gives a good run and a firm jumping-off ground, the road of tested, scientific knowledge. The scientist uses it whatever his science may be. The faith which a scientist uses is not a projection from fancy but from all he already knows and has tried and proved. In the case of the *modern*, Christian faith will be a projection from all that he knows from all possible *reliable* sources of knowing. Theology will help. The Bible will help. The experiences of the saints are scientific evidence. His own devotional discoveries and thinking will all help to make a firm road which leads to the place from which the leap of faith can best be made.

Even the mathematician uses faith. When he says that because A equals B and B equals C, that therefore A equals C, he makes a wild leap before his conclusion is reached. It is faith in the reliability of his own mental processes. Sir Oliver Lodge said of Newton, "He had an extraordinary faculty for guessing correctly sometimes with no apparent data." A glorious guess based on all that is already known is often a fairly accurate description of faith.

One of the romances of astronomical science was the discovery of the planet Neptune through a leap of faith. Proceeding along the road of scientific and tested truth, astronomers found that at one point in its vast circuit through the heavens—a revolution round the sun which takes eighty-four years—the planet Uranus swung out of its normal curve. What was it that drew that vast planet and made it alter its course? From the deviation of Uranus mathematicians actually calculated the distance, direction, and weight of the disturbing body. Its orbit was even calculated before the planet itself had been seen. Then with a glorious leap of faith astronomers swept their telescopes across the night sky and actually found Neptune, one of the outermost planets of the solar system, two thousand seven hundred and ninety-four million miles from the sun, with a period of revolution of over one hundred and sixty years. Yet to me, the deviation in the moral course of a human life owing to the fact that God has come near to that life, is in the same category of events and even more inspiring.

What, then, is faith? I should define it as the projection of the mind from what it can definitely prove toward that which is intuitively discerned. Christian faith I should define as the projection of the mind and heart from what is known already, and tested as far as may be in experience, toward that which, in response to inward quickening or vision, is spiritually apprehended.

Let me write down some other definitions.

"Faith," says Dean Inge,[1] "is not, as a schoolboy is reported to have said, believing what you know to be untrue. It is, rather, the resolution to stand or fall by the noblest hypothesis." Religion is "betting your life there's a God," said Donald Hankey. "Faith in general," says the Methodist *Catechism,* "is a conviction of the truth and reality of those things which God has revealed in the Bible. Faith in Christ is a saving grace whereby we receive him, trust in him, and rest upon him alone for salvation as he is offered to us in the gospel." "Faith means," says the author of the letter to the Hebrews,[2] "we are confident of what we hope for, convinced of what we do not see."

Now we may pass on to ask the poignant question: "How can I get the faith I need?" It may be that we need that faith definitely to overcome suffering in ourselves, to defeat and banish it. It may be that we need it to bear suffering, or—a difficult task—bear the thought of it. For in actual life one finds that those who are

[1] *Lay Thoughts of a Dean,* p. 344.
[2] Hebrews xi. 1. Moffatt.

most troubled by the mystery of pain are not the sufferers themselves but those who watch their dear ones suffer.

"Faith," says *The Oxford English Dictionary,* "is belief founded on authority." But it is fairly certain that those for whom I am writing would only accept the authority of perceived truth. Most of us cannot believe a thing which touches our life closely merely because we are told to believe it, however august the authority of the person who speaks. In the spiritual realm, at any rate, we listen respectfully while the saint or scholar speaks, and theirs is weighty evidence leading us toward faith; but the road along which we run to get our leap of faith needs, in things of the spirit, to be tested and tried and proved by us for ourselves. When the astronomer tells me that it takes a planet one hundred and sixty-five years to go round the sun, I can only accept the statement; but when I am told to believe by faith that God will forgive my sins, the matter touches me so deeply that I need to know God for myself, and glimpse, in all the ways known to me, his loving nature, before I can make the leap which lands me in a place where the soul can rest in so mighty an assertion.

In a word, faith nowadays is more readily called out if the mind runs along the road of "knowing" as far as that road can take it, rather than if it tries to make a leap from the end of the road of credulity.

This is true in the realm of healing. If I contract disease or injury, I go to my doctor. Suppose he were a saintly doctor—as, indeed, mine happens to be—and told me to kneel down and he would lay his hands upon me, I am afraid, in the case of certain injuries, that I should have little faith in the result. I sit or lie down while he patiently examines me, explains to me what is wrong and what he is going to do, and why he is going to do it, and my faith is *thus* called forth. The more I am permitted to *know,* the more easily I can produce faith in his ability to heal me. If a man has cancer, I am more likely to help his faith by telling him to take injections of a substance which a great cancer specialist has just discovered and which has cured others, than I am by telling him to carry a potato in his pocket. From the road of knowledge I can make a leap of faith. The road of credulity is no longer in good repair.

It is so in psychological work. The laying-on of hands would call forth faith far less potently with most educated people than would a simple but scientific explanation of what was wrong and what the psychologist was going to do to get it right.

Frequently a patient is badly treated by his friends. When all medical and psychological methods have failed; when osteopathy and nature-cure treatment and all the other treatments, orthodox and unorthodox, have been tried and failed, a patient is often sent to a healing mission. But if the roads of knowledge do not take him to the place whence he may make the leap of faith, it is exceedingly doubtful—unless the illness be psychogenic and the patient religiously suggestible—whether an appeal for "sheer faith" will succeed. God is being asked to make up for our ignorance of the specific nature of the patient's illness,[3] and the patient is being asked to jump where the

[3] I mean that if the patient had toothache, we should not attempt "faith healing," we should take him to the dentist. Why? Because we know what is the matter and we know what method will make him better. But whatever is the matter is knowable—capable of being discovered. And whatever should be done is discoverable. If "faith healing" is all that some claim for it, it should be applied to toothache, and dentistry would fall into disuse.

chasm is widest. It is no wonder that healing missions produce in many people black depression and hopeless despair. Most of those who attend them are not healed, and their last state is often worse than their first. The last hope is gone. The spectacle of scores of sufferers remaining unhealed depresses them far more than anything in the service helps them. The method of the laying-on of hands is irrelevant in their case. One wants them to be healed, of course; but the method of the healing mission seems, to me at any rate, a hit-and-miss method. And if the sufferers are curable by a healing mission, they are curable by a Christian psychologist who uses prayer and religious suggestion as well as other technical psychological methods. And in that private treatment the dangers of the mission as noted above are avoided. If a Christian psychologist cannot heal them, it is very unlikely that they can be healed at a mission. A temporary improvement one has seen but it is highly unsatisfactory.

A young woman known to me was lame for a number of years. After the doctors had done all they could for her she could not walk without a limp, and complained of pain. I must say, however, from personal observation, that on some days she walked *almost* without a limp. One evening she went to a "healing service," and gave the following report to the press: "I had almost to be carried on to the platform. After Pastor X had placed his hands on me and prayed I knew that I was healed.

Why should it be resorted to only when all else fails? The answer often is that we try a short cut. We try to substitute "faith" for the industry of discovering what is wrong and what should be done. But will God honor community-laziness in failing to understand and remedy illness? The suffering of thousands answers the question in the negative.

It was the most wonderful happening in my life. I walked off the platform unaided and have been able to walk without the help of anyone ever since." Following this statement in the press scores of letters flowed in from all over the country, some of them pathetic in the extreme. Should a poor woman bring her little boy from here? Should a man take a tortuous journey from there?

Unfortunately, within a few days the woman, who quite honestly thought she had been healed, was as lame as she had ever been. I directed her to write to the press and tell the facts. This she felt she could not do. I drafted a letter and asked her to send it to all her correspondents explaining that what she had said to the press she had said really believing in her own cure, but that now she must report that the cure was only a temporary alleviation such as she had had before. Whether she has done so I cannot say, as I have now lost sight of her.

I am not denying faith healing, or generalizing too much from individual cases. I have seen in my own work too many illustrations of the power of God through the mind upon the body. I am saying that in my opinion the line of approach which offers most is the road of psychological and spiritual research in the hands of those who believe in God and use the great truths about him which so wonderfully release energy in personality. The healing mission is too full of dangers to be recommended. It does not move along the road of knowing to the faith which it demands.

But I have not named the heaviest indictment against the healing mission. Here is a story founded on fact. Imagine two people as different as can be. The first is a dour, Scottish Presbyterian, a university graduate, a fine Christian who has fought for and won through to his faith in God. Further, he has a fine Christian experience. He reminds me of Tennyson's lines:[4]

> "He fought his doubts and gathered strength,
> He would not make his judgment blind,
> He faced the specters of the mind
> And laid them: thus he came at length
>
> "To find a stronger faith his own. . . ."

His mind is critical. The critical threshold is high. By this I mean that ideas are not readily received by his mind. Each idea is examined critically and accepted or rejected according to the Scot's assessment of the strength of the evidence for or against. His is not a suggestible mind.

Look at the second person. She is an uneducated and irreligious hysteric. Neither the lack of education nor the hysteria is her fault. She believes in God vaguely and dimly as such people do. She has never given ten minutes' thought to God. She has sought him neither with brain nor heart. She is suggestible. The critical threshold is low. Ideas suggested to her are, generally speaking, accepted without examination.

Let us imagine, though it is improbable, that both develop the same illness. Both are unhealed by modern medical methods. Both are persuaded to go to a healing mission. The girl is healed. The man is not.

The crowning wrong of the healing mission lies just here. The girl is praised and told she had faith. The Scot asks why he wasn't cured and is told that he hadn't faith. Both statements are dangerous lies. The girl

[4] Tennyson, "In Memoriam," XCVI.

hadn't faith. She was suggestible, that's all. The idea of healing was received, temporarily at any rate, by the mind, with the inevitable result. The Scot had a magnificent faith. But when the healer approached him, because he couldn't understand the process, and was not superstitious enough to accept what seemed irrational, he could not accept the idea of healing. But we simply must not use the phrase "faith in God" when we mean suggestibility, which is neither the fault nor the merit of the person who possesses it. Suggestibility is due to a psychological make-up which no one completely understands. It is not even based on lack of education. One of the most highly educated people I ever had to deal with was extremely suggestible. A farm laborer who came to me was found to be highly critical.

I deprecate the healing mission because it confuses in people's minds suggestibility and faith. That girl only wanted God as a means of getting better. She took the healing mission in her stride as a treatment just as she took other treatments. Now she is better, God is a nonentity, vaguely in the background as he was before. An Indian fakir could have hypnotized her and done the same trick.

When I think of the two women to whom this book is dedicated, and two women, quarrelsome and lying scandalmongers, said to have been cured by a visiting "evangelist," I claim that the "faith" of the latter does not deserve to be mentioned on the same day as that mighty faith which the former held, a faith not discredited because it did not bring the physical results hoped for; a faith maintained through all the ravages of the cancer that killed them.

If you tell me it isn't fair that one person, merely because suggestible, should be healed, and another, for lack of that mental make-up, be unhealed, I have no answer. I can only remind you that it is an old story. Every doctor will tell you that he uses a method with one patient and the patient responds. He uses the same method with the same type of illness in another patient and he is unhealed. In the case of the latter there is some inner condition, not understood, by which the therapeutic agent is resisted. Even in so simple a thing as the taking of an iron tonic we find that with one person it doesn't agree while with another it works wonders. In my own work, some people are so easily hypnotized that enormous powers can be released within them. For others hypnosis is of no avail. These are facts to be received and gradually understood. One would have to say to the Presbyterian in our story that no disparagement of his faith was involved, but that suggestion was simply not a valuable treatment in his particular case.

I am convinced that no healing today will usefully be done if its methods are far beyond an understanding of what is happening. Practical work, in this age of science, will not usefully proceed far ahead of theoretical knowledge. Our technique must not be a wild speculation but a leap of faith from the taking-off ground of scientific fact. No healing ministry, in my opinion, can have any useful function in the modern world if it despises or disparages medical, surgical, and psychological science, or attempts a short-cut method not based upon them. No doubt sporadic cures will occur, but full penalty will be paid by others, by disappointed thousands, for hopes raised that can never be realized. We must go on to more science, not to less, or we shall be back in the age of magic, supposing with the foolishness of past generations that "simple faith" is a substitute for knowledge and an excuse for the family laziness that will not use its resources.

Here I shall be met with a criticism. Jesus, it is said by many, was able to cure all manner of diseases, not merely psychogenic ones,[5] and if we believed that he was present now, all diseases would vanish before him.

My answer is that many factors have altered since then.

In the first place, although we rightly believe that Jesus is present—say at a church service—it is bound to be a less vital experience than it would be if we saw his face or heard his voice or felt his touch. We rightly sing, "We know and feel that Thou art here," but if we saw him, we shouldn't sing. The service in that form would not continue. Who would preach? All would want to kneel in adoration and bow in silence, waiting for his word. It is foreign to fact to suppose that his mediated presence has the potency of his immediate presence. It is thus no denial of piety if a patient finds he has more faith in a specialist than in Christ. He may believe in divine power working *through,* rather than independently of, human agency.

Secondly, we really know very little about the kind of cases he treated in the days of his flesh. Is it really true to assert that he healed everybody? "He healed *many* that were sick,"[6] not all. And the word translated "healed" should often be translated "treated." Luke, the doctor, uses the word which, used strictly, never meant

[5] That is, those diseases with or without physical symptoms which are originally caused in the mind by fear or conflict or some other psychological factor.
[6] Mark i. 34.

to cure, but to treat, to tend, as a doctor tends his patients. If Luke had intended to say that Jesus cured all the people who were sick, he would have used quite a different word.[7] It may have been that the difficulty lay with the patient. It does not make me reverence Christ less if I feel that there may have been some cases which he could not heal even if the patient had faith; cases, for instance, in which tissue was destroyed, such as a blindness caused by the complete destruction of the optic nerve. It may not have been God's will then, any more than now, or for Jesus any more than for us, to allow an easy short cut in the task of combating disease. He makes the health of many in the great human family depend on the skill and knowledge of others, and he may have planned that only slowly, using the resources he slowly unveils to us, should we find out how to heal certain troubles to which flesh is heir. If so, we may realize that Christ perfectly fell in with God's will. "The Son can do nothing of himself, but what he seeth the Father do."[8]

There remains the further claim that Jesus did not discriminate between psychogenic and physiogenic disease. I am not convinced about this. In the first place we have slender grounds for certainty about the type of disease he treated. And even now many diseases are looked upon as organic when their original causes may well be psychological or spiritual. If, even now, many so-called organic diseases are but the physical concomitants of psychologi-

---

[7] Compare Hugh Frame, *Wonderful Counselor,* p. 76 (Hodder & Stoughton). Luke uses medical terms strictly. In Acts 28. 8, 9 he says, "The father of Publius lay sick of a fever . . . to whom Paul entered in and prayed and laid his hands upon him and *healed* him. So when this was done, others also, which had diseases in the island, came and were *treated.*" (Two different words.)

[8] John 5. 19

cal or even spiritual disharmonies, it is possible that all the diseases Jesus cured through the faith of the patient were psychogenic, if only one could understand their ultimate origin.

But, thirdly, we must remember how different was the approach to faith in Jesus' day. Science in our sense there was none. The road was not made. The only road was credulity—the acceptance of an idea with only meager evidence. But that road was used by everybody. It was in good repair and not imperiled by the age of reasoning, not undermined by rigid scrutinies forever asking why and how. It is hopeless to ask us to go back to that now. All we can ask—and we have a right to ask it—is that science, which has destroyed credulity, should itself provide an even better road along which faith can move toward its goal.

At the same time faith in Christ was not *merely* a projection from credulity. People knew him as we do not, and their eyes saw the works he did. *Knowing* Christ was easier then than now.

If, then, the point is to be established that the most hopeful way of producing a healthy modern faith is by proceeding along the road of knowing, we must meet an objection which will be offered immediately: "If this be true, how is it that some of the cleverest men in the world are agnostic? They know a great deal, but it doesn't seem to have led them to faith."

A friend of mine, down on vacation from Oxford, confided once to his father that "no scientifically trained person could possibly be a Christian, especially one who had studied, as he had, under Professor X." It is rather pleasing to report that my friend is now one of the keenest members I know in the Oxford Group Movement, and he has led many to Christ. His keen mind was impressed by the evidence of changed lives in that movement; evidence that was scientific, and just as convincing in its own sphere as biological evidence is scientific and convincing in the sphere of biology. So often a trained mind has only to turn itself to the evidences for Christianity—and changed lives are very powerful evidences—to be convinced by them.

It is essential to make clear that by "evidences" of Christianity I do not mean only theological arguments. They have their place, those cosmological, teleological, and ontological arguments guaranteed to put some people off theology forever! The evidence that brought my student friend over to Christ's way of life so vividly and suddenly was, I think, the evidence in the lives of others of Christ's power to change them. That is scientific evidence. It is part of the road along which hundreds pass on their way to make the leap of faith for themselves.

And if certain great thinkers remain unconvinced that the claims of Christ are valid, I quite seriously put forward the view that they have never given the mental energy and concentration to the Christian position which they have given to the positions which they take up as scientists. It is pathetically true, as has often been said, that a specialist is one who knows more and more about less and less. And just as I am bound to be agnostic, say, about relativity or some other specialized subject because I have never studied it, so many a scientist moves within the orbit of his own studies and the vast subject of religion is passed by with a superior nod and a sniff.

I cannot forget that a great American scientist, once

agnostic, determined to write a book which would disprove once and for all the possibility of the resurrection of Christ. How foolish of educated people in the twentieth century to go on believing such an antiquated myth! The thing was impossible and ridiculous! Science, if it gave itself to the task, could explode it and show it to be the childish ghost story it was! But that scientist ended by writing the most convincing argument for the resurrection I have ever read. When he turned his magnificent mind to the subject and began to sift the evidence, he was convinced of its veracity. Now, he does not teach that the resurrection *may* have happened. He quotes a greater than himself and calls it the "best attested fact in history."

I can only wish that scientists who allow it to be known that they do not subscribe to the Christian faith would turn their minds to it with the devotion they have given to their own pet subjects. It would stand their scrutiny. If it won't, then the sooner that fact is known the better. None of us wants to hide in a lie. But it has stood the test of nearly two thousand years of inquiry, testing, and experience. The saints have lived by it. The doubt of the scientist is generally owing to the fact that his research into one branch of knowledge has outrun his knowledge of religion and its firm bases. It is not that the scientist knows too much. It is the fact that he doesn't know enough. The possibility of faith is not reduced by knowledge; it is increased by it. Let the specialist in biology give even a fraction of the time spent on his favorite science to the study of theology and the evidences of Christ's power and he will be convinced that Christianity is no wild dream of uneducated fanatics but based as much on living truth as any of the sciences. Men like Doctor

Temple and Doctor Inge and Doctor Barnes are not fools. The first two are philosophers. The third is a scientist. They are accredited leaders in other spheres of thought besides religion. Yet they subscribe to the Christian faith without such allegiance doing despite to their knowledge in other fields of thought. It is thought in some quarters that Christianity is irrational. The Christian is the true rationalist, for he will attend to all aspects of truth. All truth can be built into his fabric and become part of the road that leads to faith. Faith is said to have nothing to do with knowledge. Nothing could be more misleading. Faith is going a little further than actual proof or demonstration in response to intuition or vision.

Let the Christian therefore gather all the knowledge he can to make his road toward faith. Part of the evidence will be what the great theologians have argued. Theology is a science. Part of the evidence will be what the saints have experienced. Part—and an important part—will be to collect what Christ has done for men in foreign lands. Part of the evidence will consist in a survey of the lives being changed daily in this country, largely through the churches and the various group movements. Part will be the evidence of the New Testament. Most important of all, part of the evidence, even if regarded at first only as the evidence of an Expert speaking about his own subject, as Einstein might speak of relativity, is the authentic speech of Jesus. Part of the evidence will be the seeker's own impotence to become by himself what in his best moments he wants to be.

The important thing for the faith of a modern Christian is, I think, that he should know Christ as well as he can as a preliminary, before he tries to use faith as a weapon against suffering. And, frankly, this is not easy. When we are told to have the faith of a little child, it would seem to deny my theme of faith as a projection from knowledge. But there are more ways of knowing than by scientific logic; and it is beautifully true of the child that the path of knowing is not littered with pride and prejudice and presuppositions; with cynicism and material ways of looking at life. How often these things have prevented the knowledge of God which we so much need for our leap of faith!

Knowing Christ is not easy, however, even though we be childlike. If we had lived in Galilee with Jesus, knowledge of him would have been readily accessible. I think it is a perfectly fair point to make that Jesus is definitely harder to know now. Speaking of the centurion whose faith made it possible for Jesus to cure his servant, Machen says:[9] "The plain fact is that we are by no means in the same situation as the centurion was with reference to Jesus; we of the twentieth century need to know very much more about Jesus in order to trust him than the centurion needed to know. If we had Jesus with us in bodily presence now, it is quite possible that we might be able to trust him with very little knowledge indeed; the majesty of his bearing might conceivably inspire unbounded confidence almost at first sight. But, as a matter of fact, we are separated from him by nineteen centuries; and if we are to commit ourselves unreservedly to a Jew who lived nineteen hundred years ago, as to a living person, there are obviously many things about him that we need to know. For one thing, we need to know that he is

[9] *What is Faith?* p. 91, J. Gresham Machen, D.D. The Macmillan Company, New York.

alive; we need to know, therefore, about the resurrection. And then we need to know how it is that he can touch our lives; and that involves a knowledge of the atonement and of the way in which he saves us from our sin. But it is useless to enter into further detail. Obviously, it is a very strange thing that persons of the twentieth century should come into a relation of living trust with a Man of the first century; and if they are to do so, they must know much more about him than his contemporaries needed to know. Even if the centurion, therefore, could get along with very little knowledge of the person of Christ, it does not follow that we can do so." "It is impossible," says the same writer,[10] "to have faith in a person without having knowledge of the person; far from being contrasted with knowledge, faith is founded upon knowledge."

I am often troubled by the querulous people who come to me in some distress or another, and they say, "I *have* prayed to God and I *do* trust God." "I've gone to church all my life," they wail, "and I say my prayers night and morning," but many of them only want God to get them right. They don't want God for his own sake. They have made no serious quest to get into that joyous relationship with God of the child to the loving father. They want God as they want anything—a tonic or an operation; or any other kind of treatment would do which would give them health or ease. They would probably proceed to forget him again or let him fade vaguely into the conventional background of a so-called religious life which never has had the real, vital, infectious experience, but has only had a conventional substitute, a dreary fake, a

[10] *Ibid.*, p. 46.

bleak self-deception, a misery-producing tyranny which, so far from making religion attractive, would put another definitely off so mournful a possession.

If we have made no effort to know God, we cannot suddenly develop faith in him because we are ill or in trouble. We must put ourselves to school and come to desire God and know God for his own sake and not merely for the good things we can get out of him.

When we do know God as he is, we can produce a faith, projected from knowledge, which really can sustain us. It may, indeed, bring us health again. It may not, for reasons which have been put before the reader earlier in this book. But it will bring us more than health. It will mean that we can bear with equanimity the loss of health. It will mean that we can even use our suffering and pain to his glory. The fact thus established is that which lands us in the country of desire—not merely that of personal health, but personal communion, which is the highest thing man can possibly know on earth. If we have that, then everything else falls into a new perspective, and those things which are hurting us most can be seen to be relatively unimportant.

It cannot be too often repeated that the highest faith in God is not that which is tested merely by the things we hope to get through the exercise of faith, not even health, no, not even salvation. The highest faith can be measured not by such results, but by the depth and richness of the communion with God which follows every leap of faith from the end of the road of knowing. And at that edge stands One who, as we leap, puts his scarred hand under our elbow and gives us a power which carries us further than any leap of our own could bring us. The power of Christ is released into the soul at the moment of its leap.

Our conclusion, therefore, is that the first necessity of faith is a deeper knowledge of God and of his Son Jesus Christ; a knowledge, I repeat, which is partly reached by the study of theology and the perception of truth thus arrived at. For myself I think it is difficult to exaggerate the value of making the mind, week after week, take time to study and understand the ways of God to man. Few things can be more important than to know what the most enlightened minds of our age are telling us about the nature of God and his work in the world.

But God is known also in other ways—the inner light, the devotional experience, the touch of beauty, the warm glow of truth perceived as well as reached through logical argument; the manifestation of his nature through the goodness of men and women and the love of a little child; the biblical revelation and the stern message of history; the observation of God's ways in the laboratory and in the majestic march of planets through the sky. In countless ways God can be known, and the more he is known the more is a strong faith possible.

Here is a young man in an English university. He has faith in his father, who lives in Australia, and sends him a very occasional letter and a check to pay his bills. How different is the case of a young man at a university whose father lives in a neighboring city! The father writes to his boy and pays his bills; but every holiday, and many a time between, they meet face to face. There is a cheery knock on the door and the young man comes into his father's study and says, "I say, Dad, tell me what to do about this and that." The two have constant communion. They know each other thoroughly, and the son's faith has a different quality.

If you decide to think of God as an absentee Deity, dwelling somewhere beyond all worlds, whom you decide you will ring up occasionally when you are in trouble and ask his advice, and whom you expect, as it were, to pay your bills and get you out of any mess into which you may fall, I think you will find faith difficult. But if you will think of God as a Father, not even in the next room, but in the same room as yourself, loving, caring, intimate, friendly, to whom you may turn in joys and sorrows, who may not "get you out of the mess" but who passes through all your troubles with you, ready and able to turn each one into a sacrament, then you will find faith one of the richest things in life.

This is what God desires. "Before they call," he says, "I will answer," and he leans out of his immensity toward you, my reader, and of you he says, "I will be his God and he shall be my son."

But there is still one very important aspect of our subject which we have left undiscussed. It is the strength of the vision which calls out our faith. In imagination we have seen a man running along a road, tried and tested, and, from the end of it, making a leap of faith from a cliff edge on to a rocky islet standing in the sea. And it has been suggested that the modern leap of faith is best made by taking a run along the road of knowing. But we have made no allowance for the kindling vision of the glory of the islet which puts power into his spring. We might almost call this part of our subject, "Look before you leap," because the vision of that to which faith reaches out can strengthen faith a hundredfold.

Modern psychology is very insistent concerning the picture of himself which a man allows his mind to foster. A lot depends on what a man's own picture of himself in his heart of hearts is. It is very important, of course, that a man's faith in himself should be based on reality. In other words, that he should not have exaggerated ideas of his abilities out of all proportion to the facts. Here again faith in himself must be based on knowledge of himself. At the same time, that being granted, it is very, very important that a man's imaginative picture of himself should be a picture of a person succeeding, not a picture of a person failing, a picture of health, not a picture of disease.

Again and again, in our contact with people, we find that a man of splendid possibilities fails only because his mental picture is that of a man failing. And we do not need Coué to tell us that any amount of forcing of the will is unable to defeat the power of the dominant imaginative picture. Man rises to his greatest abilities when imagination and will are both urging him the same way; that is, when he is saying, at the same time, "I will and I can," for if he says, "I will but I cannot," or even, "I am afraid I cannot," then the power of the imagination to defeat him is overwhelmingly greater than the energy of the will prompting him to success. It is almost ludicrous to realize that intensity of effort seems powerless to bring us where we most earnestly want to be, if still, underneath all our effort, the mind retains a mental picture of failure.

Like so much more of the new psychology we find all this in the New Testament. Saint Paul says, "The good which I would I do not, but the evil which I would not, that I do."[11] "To will is present with me but to do is not." But he says, "I can do all things in him that strengtheneth me." Here is a remarkable testimony to a well-known psychological fact, that the will is an over-estimated source of achievement unless it is fired by what could be called imaginative confidence. It is absolutely essential for the soul to say, "I can."

Probably we are familiar with Coué's picture of a plank only eighteen inches wide, lying on the ground. Almost anybody could walk along it, but raise it to the height of cathedral towers and few could do so. Yet the plank is the same width and the will has not been altered. The difference surely is that when the plank is on the ground, we can make a mental picture of ourselves succeeding. When the plank is at a great height from the ground, our mental picture is of ourselves falling. Therefore, though we will to do a thing we at the same time say "I cannot," and failure is certain. I have elaborated the point elsewhere and need not do so again now.[12]

The whole art of autosuggestion or heterosuggestion is directed toward bringing the mind to the habit of making a mental picture of itself as it desires to be. Then faith can be called out, achievement seems possible, the heart sings "I can," the will says "I will," and this mental picture of achievement is one of the most important things by which success is attained. "Every day in every way I am getting better and better." If, day after day, a person with any illness in the world is saying "Oh, dear, I am just as bad as ever I was, and probably worse"—and we all know people who seem to hate admitting the slightest

[11] Romans 7. 19.
[12] *Psychology and Life*, p. 85. The Abingdon Press.

improvement—then the energies which can bring health are, to some extent, dammed up. If, on the other hand, the mind is looking toward recovery, believing in recovery, cherishing a mental picture of the personality as completely restored, then those energies are most certainly flowing toward recovery.

Saint Mark alone has preserved for us a most thrilling sentence from the lips of Jesus: "All things whatsoever ye pray and ask for, believe that ye have received them, and ye shall have them."[13] So that when, by prayer and faith, we are longing for something, we are to hold in our mind the picture of ourselves possessing it. Those are the conditions under which we can make it ours. I have wondered whether Saint Paul did not mean the same kind of thing when to the Romans he says, "Reckon ye also yourselves to be dead unto sin, but alive unto God in Christ Jesus."[14] He is talking to people who are troubled with all sorts of sins, and he is asking them to make a picture of themselves free from them and cleansed from them. "See yourself," he says, "without all these horrible things about you, and let that vision inspire you to make it true."

Our conclusion is that whatever faith desires can be best attained by proceeding along the road of knowing as far as that road will take us, and making our leap with, as I suggest, a Hand under our elbow which gives us the final thrust, but behind and underneath all our effort we are to hold always definitely in the mind the vision of that which we want to reach. If it is health, then the vision of ourselves healed. If it is the health of another, then

[13] Mark 11. 24.
[14] Romans 6. 11.

the vision of him completely healed. If it is the success in this direction or another, then we are to hold in the mind the vision of the thing as though it were already achieved. If it is sin to be conquered, then added to all our fighting and effort we are to hold the vision of ourselves cleansed. It is so very important that the picture of oneself in one's own mind should be a picture of the person one desires to be, the picture of the person Christ can make one.

Now, this is surely where imagination comes in. Imagination is not to be despised as a faculty which is only useful to portray the fanciful. It has that glorious use, and we must all be grateful to men like Barrie, Stevenson, Milne, Lewis Carroll, and the rest; to the great artists of the brush as well as of the pen, who can lift us out of dullness and soberness into flights of imaginative fancy. But I want to make it clear that the imagination is not only a faculty by which we can make pictures of what does not exist. It is also a faculty by which we can apprehend a reality which is unseen. And within its own sphere it is as valuable a way of reaching reality as, shall we say, sight or logic.

As soon as one begins to talk about imagination in religion some people suppose that what is imagined cannot be there. It is important to assert that some realities can be apprehended only by the imagination. The force of gravity is one. No one has ever seen it. I can only *imagine* a pull from the earth's center which draws all things thereto. Of course I can imagine things that are not there at all. I can imagine fairies. But gradually in experience I can test out what I have imagined, and experience, in time, will give the lie to what is nonexistent.

But do let us remember that, again and again, faith begins by an act of imagination.

The faith of a little child is often wholly in the imagination. He imagines, when he says his prayers, that Jesus is present, tall and dark, with kind eyes, a figure dressed in Eastern robes, perhaps, putting a hand on his bowed head. "Imagination," you say, "just as he imagines fairies." Yes, but in the case of the fairies he surrenders his faith in time, because it is not vindicated in experience. But that little baby faith in Jesus, while it undergoes modifications when tested by reality, endures, and may become one of the strongest factors in his life. He still imagines Jesus, but the something imagined is not nonexistent. Imagination is a reliable faculty by which the unseen can be apprehended.

In point of fact, any means by which the imagination can be helped to picture Jesus is a definite help to faith, because it is this kind of mental picture which calls forth faith. One imagines Jesus in a hut on a hillside, and oneself allowed to speak to him there.[15] Or one imagines Jesus sitting in a chair opposite one and oneself talking to him as a man talks to his friend.[16] They are imaginative pictures but they cannot be dismissed as "only imagination," because they paint a picture of that to which faith is reaching out, namely, the communion of the soul with Christ; and faith is ten times more potent when there is already painted in the mind a picture of what faith is seeking.

The more faith grows, the more it is directed not toward things, not even worthy things, but toward Christ.

[15] *Jesus and Ourselves*, p. 255. The Abingdon Press.
[16] *The Transforming Friendship*, p. 46. The Abingdon Press.

The more faith grows, it does not say, "Give me," it says, "Make me." The more faith grows, it does not strive nor cry, it makes the communion of the soul with God its first quest, whether gifts, like health, follow or whether they be withheld.

One of the loveliest illustrations of what I mean is found, strangely enough, in our old friend the twenty-third psalm. There is no agonized cry to God to give this and to do that. There, quietly, and in marvelous language, with poetic insight and spiritual apprehension, and with (and this is most important) *the use of the present tense,* the soul is asserting to itself that what it needs *is happening;* the soul is painting the vision, as true now, of what it wants to attain. Not, "O Lord, be my shepherd," but "The Lord *is* my shepherd; I shall not want." "He is making me to lie down in green pastures; he is leading me beside still waters. He is restoring my soul. He is guiding me in the paths of righteousness for his name's sake."

The miracle of Christianity, a miracle which, to my mind, far outsoars even the miracles of the days of his flesh, is the present offer of the friendship of Jesus. Through all the ages he offers himself to every man.

Let faith set that vision in front of it, let the eye of the soul be held by it, let the mind paint a picture of personality always in touch with that radiant Presence, and itself dwelling in a communion with Christ which ever becomes richer and deeper. Then according to our faith it shall be done unto us. And to dwell with that Presence is to be transformed, whatever happens to brother body, for that transforming friendship is the greatest regenerating influence the world has ever known.

CHAPTER XI[1]

IS THE UNIVERSE JUSTIFIABLE?

THE work of Professor Eddington, Sir James Jeans, and others has opened up to us a new universe. Thanks to the wireless and the popular nature of some of the books of the latter author, those who have had no training in physics can glimpse the vastness of the universe in which we seem to be such tiny specks. I picked up *The Mysterious Universe,* and before I had read a word my eye lighted on a photograph, inserted as a frontispiece, of a minute piece of the sky taken with the largest telescope in the world. The little points of light shown on the photograph are nebulae at such a distance from us that their light, traveling one hundred and eighty-six thousand miles a second, takes fifty million years to reach the earth. Then I learn that these nebulae are not stars, but the stuff from which stars are made. Each contains some thousands of millions of stars, and about two million of these nebulae can actually be photographed; and Sir James says there are millions of others beyond the reach of any telescope.

As we look up on a lovely starlit night, the sky seems full of stars; but Sir James says that if we could empty Waterloo Station of everything except six specks of dust—it would still be more crowded with dust than space is with stars.

---

[1] Part of this chapter was published as a booklet called *The Guarded Universe.* That part has been rewritten, but is reproduced here by permission of the publishers, Hodder & Stoughton, Ltd., London.

When we look at that dust beneath our feet, we little realize that in a single grain of sand there are marvels as amazing as those above our heads. "If a dewdrop," says Sir Oliver Lodge, "were expanded to the size of a planet, the molecules in it would still be no bigger than footballs." Within those molecule-footballs are atoms, which he compares with oranges, and for many years those atoms were thought to be the smallest conceivable parts of an element. But we are now taught that within the atom are electrons, which revolve round their nucleus several thousand million times a second, with a speed of hundreds of miles a second. One imagines these electrons packed tightly within the atoms, but in another of his books Sir Oliver Lodge corrects this mistake and says that an electron has as much room to move within the atom as a bee has to move in Saint Paul's Cathedral.

So whether we look up or down we find the new physics introducing us to a universe which staggers the imagination. But as I have pondered over these things I have seen the shining of a truth which to me throws light on the problem of suffering; a truth which brought my own mind out to a place of peace.

Whether we call a thing a discovery of science or whether we call it a revelation of God is mainly a matter of point of view. No scientist *could* discover anything unless God revealed it; and progress in scientific research might equally accurately be called the progressive revelation of God. If we turn back through the great discoveries of science, we find an interesting fact: that man has never discovered anything until he has been within sight of ability to deal with the situation made by the discovery. I say "within the sight of," because we remember that when Copernicus said that the sky was *not* an inverted basin over the earth, with stars, as it were, stuck on the inside of it, he was ridiculed; and when Galileo said that the earth moved round the sun and could no longer be regarded as the center of the universe, he was made to recant. So afraid are men of being led beyond the comfortable familiarity of the known. But both the truths of Copernicus and of Galileo came to stay. It is an impressive fact that man has only been allowed to discover the facts about the universe when he is able to bear them and handle the situation which they create. There have always been X-rays, there has always been radium, and God must have longed for men to have the use of these beneficent discoveries; but he did not reveal them; or, putting it the other way, man did not discover them until he was in sight of ability to control them. Man has not always controlled them wisely. He has often grievously misused those powers which have come into his hands. Many of us recall some of the horrors of the Great War as evidence of this fact. Poison gas, for instance, is a misuse of discoveries men ought to be using for social instead of antisocial purposes. Man has *power* to handle vast forces for the building up of civilization just as he has power to do the opposite. One of the great problems of the age is whether man *will* handle the available power rightly. As Mr. Julian Huxley says, "The problem of what man will do with the enormous possibilities of power which science has put into his hands is probably the most vital and alarming of modern times." And Sir Oliver Lodge once expressed the wish that we might have a truce of fifty years in scientific discovery, in order to give man a last chance to raise his moral standard to the stature of these terrific discoveries and energies. Unless he does this, of course, disaster will overtake this civilization. It will go down in a catastrophe greater than our power to imagine. To put story upon story on a new building without deepening foundations may look like development. In reality it is bringing catastrophe nearer and nearer. No one can view the increase in our knowledge of resources and vast energies without some anxiety as to whether the spiritual development is proceeding sufficiently. "It is better," someone has truly said, "to arrive at the station in a horse and trap than to arrive in the ditch in a Rolls Royce." There must be adequate control of the forces operating, or it might even be better not to have discovered the forces.

But my point here is that nothing has burst upon man which he was *incapable* of controlling. If this had not been true, one of two disasters would have happened. Firstly, man might have lost his reason, since the shock of the discovered forces would have been too much for the brain. We can see this clearly if we imagine that we could call back our great-great-grandfather and put him down at midnight in Piccadilly Circus, London, or Times Square, New York. His mind would not be tuned in to such a fast-moving world, so full of distraction. He would almost lose his sanity. The second alternative could be compared with the position of a child on board a locomotive going at eighty miles an hour. There would be tremendous forces operating and insufficient power to control them. Instead of either alternative, revelation, or, if you like, discovery, is held back until the situation which is opened up can be handled.

Now, all this is true of the psychical sphere, which is just as much part of the universe as is the physical. It is made a *uni*verse by the one Mind controlling all. We often feel that we get very near the edge of what the human mind can bear. The wall between the universe that we can bear and the universe we could not bear is very thin, but it is there. I want to suggest a picture which lights up what I mean. Imagine a camp in the deserts of Mesopotamia. Imagine it to be completely surrounded by very efficient sentries. Nothing can get in from outside, nothing can get out from within the camp, unless the sentries allow it. Of course, it is possible to creep up behind the sentries and, at dusk, to see the ghostly forms of Arab raiders out there in the gloom. But one can go back to one's tent and sleep in perfect security because the sentries are so efficient. Nothing can break in from outside unless it passes the sentries; and though, in the course of time, the sentries advance into the desert, bringing more and more of it into the camp, it never gets too big to be efficiently worked.

The universe we know and can bear is the camp. But it is guarded universe. God has put sentries round it. Nothing can come in unless it passes them. Nor can anything get out. The sentries never fail in their duty. The universe extends as discovery after discovery takes place. The sentries advance into the desert. But always they maintain their formation. Always completely they encircle the camp. And they do not go so quickly as to cause alarm. The camp is always manageable.

At the same time just beyond the sentries is the universe we could not bear. If you have heard a master violinist, you will know what I mean. He can sometimes take you through all the lovely sounds we know, and then, on and upward till his violin is sobbing and yearning and agonizing like the voice of humanity crying out in the wilderness of the infinite with no language but a cry. We feel we can bear no more. We nearly cry out to him to stop. But he stops. Why? Because he cannot go further. He has come to the edge of the universe we can bear, and a sentry's arm is across his path.

Take the normal man's belief in regard to ghosts. He may pretend he does not believe in them at all. But he does. If he says he doesn't, I would like to get him into my study at eleven o'clock at night and tell him three stories; then make him go and stand in a churchyard while it struck twelve! I am quite serious in this suggestion. I think I am as hard to convince as most people. I want evidence. I want the exclusion of all alternative hypotheses. I know that the history of psychical research has some queer chapters in it. But it seems to me irrational to refuse the evidence of trained scientific observers like Sir Oliver Lodge, Sir William Barrett, Mr. Drayton Thomas, Mr. J. Arthur Hill, and others, and to pretend that the findings of the Society for Psychical Research are, what a friend of mine once called, "a lot of bunkum about spooks." I am myself convinced that there is a psychic universe just beyond the one we know. It is the universe we could not bear in its plenitude, but it is there.

Some of my friends who have themselves made explorations into the phenomena of spiritualism give me the same impression. I stayed once with an eminent Judge, a K.C., who had himself witnessed what are called poltergeist phenomena. Things would fly about the room, books jump out of the bookcase, vases drop off the mantelpiece. And though there may be an alternative theory in regard to the vases—for we too have had some exciting maids in our time—there was no doubt why the learned Judge gave up spiritualism. Late one night he assured me, with real fear in his eyes and voice, that he gave up the whole thing because he felt he was on the threshold of a universe which he could not bear to know. The better type of spiritualists have got right up to the walls of the universe we know. They have tapped on them, and something or someone seems to tap from the other side. No doubt there is another universe on the other side, but there is a wall between them, because as yet we could not bear any more, and spiritualistic progress is slow because our minds are tuned in to this known universe and find it hard to react normally to another. I quote, with permission, two letters from the London *Times* of April, 1931, showing the power of animals to sense a universe beyond our own.

To the Editor of the *Times.*
Sir:

The following experience may be of interest to your readers on account of the exactness with which the point in space which held the dog's interest was defined.

Some years ago I possessed a bob-tailed sheep-dog, and was returning with him from a walk by way of a path which led from the road to the bottom of the garden. On one side of this path was a thin laurel hedge through which it was easy to see the lane beyond. On the other side was an iron railing, separating the path from a field. It was evening, but still broad daylight. On entering the path the dog stopped and pointed. I went on, thinking he had seen some cat, but as he did not follow, I turned and called him. His eyes were fixed upon a certain point on the path in front of him, and, as I called, they moved hesitatingly from this point to me and back again. Presently he came on, with obvious reluctance, squeezing himself against the railings at this particular point, as if there were scarcely room for him to pass. All the time his gaze was fixed on the empty space which he was passing, and, once clear of it, he bolted up to me. Then he turned, looking fixedly back at the same spot again. I walked back and called him from the other end of the path, whereupon he repeated his tactics, squeezing himself against the railings at exactly the same spot again, and never taking his eyes off the invisible something which he evidently saw in the path.

When, after seven repetitions of this, the dog turned for the last time to gaze, I saw his head and eyes moving slowly to the right. He was obviously watching whatever it was, moving away across the field. After this he passed the place as usual.

The interest of this case lies in the fact that the direction of the dog's gaze from both sides, combined with the spot at which he squeezed himself against the railings, marked down the position of what he saw to an inch. To me it was just empty space.

Your obedient servant,

To the Editor of the *Times*.
Sir:

Some years ago I took a valuable bull-terrier bitch, which was shortly due to have puppies, to Jehangir's tomb, which is situated some short distance from Lahore. On the way there a member of the party observed that my bitch had a look of apprehension or foreboding which was foreign to her. I was forced to agree with the truth of this statement, but attributed her appearance to her approaching maternity and thought nothing more about it. I should add that at this time she was taking herself very seriously and was disinclined for any but the most leisured and sedate exercise.

On our arrival at the tomb she was not allowed inside

but when we paid our visit the custodian of the tomb suggested that she should accompany us up to the large flat roof of the tomb, from which a view of the countryside could be obtained. He added, however, that the tomb was haunted by the spirit of the dead ruler—a Mohammedan. No sooner had we ascended the broad steps to the roof than my bitch, although quite accustomed to being on roofs of a like character, ran quickly to the nearest parapet, which was some two feet in height, and literally hurled herself over it. She was killed instantly. I cannot but feel convinced that some guardian spirit of the dead made itself apparent to cause this panic and consequent self-destruction.

But my tale continues. Within three months another bull-terrior bitch—in the same condition as mine—belonging to Colonel X, I.M.S., did exactly the same thing, and hurled herself to destruction from the opposite side of the tomb. I had no idea Colonel X was going to visit the tomb and only heard of his tragedy on the following day.

I am, Sir,
Yours faithfully,

After a summarized form of this argument had appeared in print a correspondent contributed the following:

In one of our circuits we lived in a semidetached house and we kept two dogs, a collie setter and a pug. A widowed lady lived alone next door. She was very house proud and particularly fond of pictures. She used to buy them at the sale rooms at Blackpool and was heard to say that when she died she would certainly come back sometimes to look at them. Mrs. B. had a tragic end. She went to Blackpool, purchased a very large fine picture and brought it home with her. The picture was packed in a luggage cart and nothing would do but Mrs. B. must follow on foot. She had a weak heart and when hurrying up the hill so as to be in time to see the picture unpacked, she collapsed in the road, was taken to a house near, and died before the doctor arrived. Of course there was an inquest, and after the funeral a sale of the effects, and the house was closed and looked very desolate.

One evening Mr. C. and I were sitting over the fire on his return from a long tramp to a country appointment, when we heard the sound of water running in the next house. My husband said, "I must go and see what is wrong." We had the key, the maids had gone to bed, it was after eleven o'clock, so I said I would go too. We took the dogs with us and a lighted candle. We found the stop tap and turned off the water and were ready to leave the house when we noticed something very peculiar about the dogs, they were so uneasy. The kitchen door opened into a long hall with the front door at the other end. The dogs went into the hall and then suddenly stopped annd gazed in front of them. Then the pug, which did not know Mrs. B., turned tail and rushed back to us trembling in every limb. But Carlo, the large dog (he had been very fond of Mrs. B., and was often in her house), put his head on one side and slowly wagged his tail, but did not advance any further. Of course we saw no one, but it seemed as though the dogs did. It was very uncanny and I was glad to go back home. The dogs seemed scared and were glad to get out of the house.

It is not hard to believe that Balaam's ass saw some-one in her path[2] after incidents like these.

Jesus was sure of the universe just beyond our own. "Thinkest thou," he said to Peter in an hour of great need,[3] "that I cannot beseech my Father and he shall even now send me more than twelve legions of angels?" Dr. Rendel Harris, one of the foremost living scholars of the New Testament, tells us, in his book *As Pants The Hart,* that it is clear that for a moment Jesus was looking into a world which he knew even better than this

---

[2] Numbers 22. 23.
[3] Matthew 26. 53.

one. Here were twelve men with him, eleven of them runaways, and one a traitor. Suppose each man were replaced by a whole legion of angels. How the kings of the earth would hide themselves in caves and in holes of the rocks before the glory of the Lord! But it was only for a moment. "Put up thy sword!" It might have been the word to those waiting hosts, eager to burst through, as well as to Peter. But Jesus ordered the sentries to halt those legions and turn them back. With them he could drive out all his enemies—at the cost of their sanity. And Jesus loved his enemies. Caiaphas and Pilate might have been made to bow to him—and be lunatics for life. No, the legions must be turned back. Nothing which would make a situation man cannot handle must pass the sentries.

Peter, at the transfiguration, got close to the walls of the universe we can bear. He looked beyond them and saw Moses and Elijah talking with Jesus. In his words, "Let us make three booths,"[4] we see certain symptoms of a mind distressed by the uncanny: "Let me do something with my hands." "For he wist not what to say, for they became sore afraid." Nor perhaps is it accidental that the evangelist records that at the climax of their horror "there came a cloud overshadowing them," blotting out from them the universe they could not bear. It was with the utmost relief that, when Peter lifted up his face at the words of Jesus, "Arise, be not afraid,"[5] he saw no one but Jesus only.

When we turn to the spiritual universe, the same glorious fact holds. Nothing will be *allowed* to come to us save that with which we have power to deal, however

[4] Mark 9. 5.
[5] Matthew 17. 7.

strange or uncanny or terrifying it may seem. We have tried to distinguish in our minds between what God allows and what he intends. He allows sin. He does not intend sin. He allows it because the risk it involves is worth the prize of a voluntarily chosen morality. As Doctor Temple said at Oxford recently, "the capacity for sin and for communion with God are the same capacity." He allows calamity. He does not deal it out to us. But it would not be *allowed* at all, unless we had power to handle the situation which arises from it.

Therefore—and it is a triumphant "therefore"—the measure of the so-called calamity is the measure of God's trust in us to use our resources, and less than the measure of gain that may be won from the calamity. The calamity would not be allowed to break through unless this were true.

Suppose a man had enough money to furnish an ideal nursery for his children. He would not make it like a padded room in an asylum. He would, if he had children like mine, guard the fire and bar the window. He would not allow safety-razor blades to be left on the floor. Otherwise a situation might arise with which he could not deal. It would, however, be possible for a child to get a pretty bad bump in the nursery, but the father knows that he and his child can handle the situation together and that good can come out of it—courage and understanding of the nature of things.

The universe is God's nursery and we are children in it. And it is guarded. We can get a very bad bump in it. We can lose our money, our health, our loved ones. In this universe a sinless Man can die on a cross. But nothing can happen physically or psychically or spiritually unless we are in sight of power to handle it and bring good from it. So whenever we look at a calamity—cancer, for instance—we must say, "The measure of this calamity must be the measure of my faith, since it is less than the measure of God's purpose." To be resentful at calamity is to show the same disbelief which tortured heretics and burned witches at the stake: to be unrealistic to such an extent that a situation can arise which we dare not contemplate with quiet faith. Though a very hard saying, it is a lack of faith to be unable to bear the thought of anything which God allows.

Bishop Selwyn changed the pigsty into which the Maoris cast him into a place where he could worship God, until they said in amazement, "It is impossible to degrade a man like this." John Nelson changed into a paradise the dungeon under a slaughterhouse into which he was cast. He wrote, "It stank worse than a hog-sty by reason of the blood and filth that flowed into it from above." Then he adds these words, "My soul was so filled with the love of God that it was a paradise to me." Bunyan changed Bedford jail into a Palace Beautiful. Michael Fairless changed a sick-room of pain into a window through which the world might see the fair face of nature and the glory of God.

It was this amazing alchemy that puzzled Pliny, when, in the famous letter to Trajan, the story of the brave Christian prisoner standing arraigned before the furious Roman magistrate was told. "I will banish thee," said the magistrate. "Thou canst not," was the reply, "the whole world is my Father's house." "I will slay thee," said the magistrate. "Thou canst not," was the reply, "for my life is hid with Christ in God." "I will take away thy treasures." "Thou canst not," he answered, "for my treasure is in heaven." "I will drive thee away from man and thou shalt have no friend left." "Thou canst not," said the Christian, "for I have a Friend from whom thou canst not separate me." There is nothing more such a soul can fear. He has reached the final harbor where the mind can rest and the soul is safe. When the soul gets there, nothing can touch it any more.

It may be the same for us. Take hold of the difficult situation with both hands and let God show his way in that situation; follow that and you will win through. Jesus will show us how to turn blood-stained wood into finest gold, thorns into crowns, and a cross into a throne.

This is a guarded universe. Nothing can overtake us which we are not able to bear. If sometimes we are overwhelmed by the thought of this vast universe of which we seem to be such unimportant specks, we must think of ourselves as princes, overwhelmed by the vastness, splendor, and intricacies of the palace and its life. But the palace is our Father's home and our Father's guards are around it. And nothing can touch us without our Father's knowledge. Always we may hold fast to our Father's hand. If we could but realize this truth, it would take fear from both life and death, for death is only the passage into another room in the Father's house.

Sings Whittier,

> "I know not where his islands lift
> Their fronded palms in air,
> I only know I cannot drift
> Beyond his love and care."

We might add: "I know not where his nebulae burn

in the abyss of space. I know not how his electrons whirl round their nucleus in the atoms of a grain of sand. I know not the psychic habitat of ghosts nor the realms of discarnate spirits. I know not what I may be called upon to bear." But no ship can sail off the ocean; and all the oceans on which we can sail are in the hollow of his hand.

> ". . . I *cannot* drift
> Beyond his love and care."

So we may feel at home in our Father's world and know that the universe is so guarded that nothing can break through which has any inherent power to smash us or destroy the purpose of our lives. There is a limit set to suffering, and he will not ask from us more than we are able to bear. The measure of our suffering is the measure he himself has sanctioned and allowed. The dread angels of suffering can pass the sentries, for God gave them the countersign which brings them through. Their credentials are in order. We must "suffer them to be so now." God suffers at their hands himself. But our reaction—ah, that is another matter! It can be resentment, bitterness, and despair. But by his help and grace it can be spiritual power, making the world his more than ever, and giving to us a treasure which no mind can reckon and which no hand can take away.

CHAPTER XIII

IS DEATH A CALAMITY?

AT Manchester I had the privilege of meeting an exceptionally brilliant man with whom I had a conversation that lasted far into the night. The question that was on his mind could be stated like this: "How do you know that the soul goes on; and even if it does, why are we subjected to this terrifying experience of dying?" A book which seeks to give help with the problem of suffering ought to have a chapter on what have been called "the pains of death." For it is true to say that he who has not contemplated the problem of death has never contemplated life deeply. A working-class woman told a friend that she had listened to a youth of nineteen criticizing the present world-order and religious situation. This was wrong, and that was wrong. She silenced him with the following surprising and seemingly irrelevant remark: "Young man, you will think differently on many matters when you have stood by a deathbed." This was not a mere damping of youthful ardor, but a very wise remark, for the fact of death is one of the hardest facts of life and must be faced by any person who would make his view complete.

I therefore want to face now "this business of dying." I hope to write later a few paragraphs about the vast subject of immortality; but first of all let us recognize how many people there are who can contemplate entry into another world, with joy, but it is the thought of the dreadful valley between, which daunts them. Even Bunyan dreaded it and called it "a horror and a great darkness." I have had the confidence of so many people who are brave in regard to suffering but terrified at the thought of dying, that I would like to offer them some good news.

Let us collect some evidence. Surely, it is a wise way, in trying to face any particular problem, to collect all the available evidence, and then, whatever deductions we make, they will be well based. I give my own testimony first, because it is the least important, and I want to say, at once, that in my experience as a minister and army chaplain, an experience covering about twenty years, I must have seen scores of people dying, and I have never known the actual moment of passing to be marked by any kind of terror or anxiety. It has always been a peaceful and beautiful thing. Scores of doctors and ministers whom I have consulted say the same thing. Of course, everyone will recognize that in a large number of cases unconsciousness supervenes before death occurs. But when a person passes out with his conscious life maintained until the end, the evidence is simply overwhelming that death is a beautiful experience, though we have for so long been intimidated into an opposite belief. I have seen people, for instance, who for many weary weeks could not lift their heads from the pillow, sit up at the moment of death and stretch out their arms, with a smile of utter rapture on their faces. I have heard people, again and again, breathe the name of someone who had passed over before them. One friend with whom I sat, kept saying, almost under his breath, "How beautiful it looks through the gates," and he gave one the impression of a person pressing on to some unbelievably beautiful experience. He spoke repeatedly of flowers. My own sister, thought to be dying of pneumonia, told me that she understood that they did not expect her to live, and she couldn't understand their tears, for she was wrapped in an incredible sense of well-being, with marvelous music sounding in her ears. At last she heard someone say, "She's going to get better," and she felt distinct disappointment at being pulled back from a delightful prospect. Convalescence, she said afterward, was sheer misery! She told me that she looked at her loved ones with a kind of incredulous smile, as one who would say, "You may call this getting better, but it is a very dull experience compared with the one I nearly entered." I do not imply, of course, actual "gates of heaven" or "music," but impressions which got through to human consciousness in that form. I will not occupy too much space with a large number of similar cases, but I should like to quote two more.

A well-known journalist, Mr. W. C. Edgar, wrote an article in *The Spectator*[1] called "The Adventure of Dying." He tells how he was advised to have a very dangerous operation, although at the time, as far as he knew, he was in perfectly good health. He thus went to the operation in a condition far different from the exhausted body and mind of many patients. He had a local anaesthetic, and as he lay on the table he said to himself: "I am going to bring to this occasion the instincts of my craft. This is a very interesting event, in which I am going to take the leading part. I am about to enter the famous 'valley of the shadow of death,' and few have

[1] February 11, 1928.

returned therefrom to tell the tale. My wits are all about me, I am not drugged into unconsciousness. I am able to see and hear and reason clearly, and will be to the end. I am going to make careful notes of this adventure and afterward set down all its details." He then goes on to describe the sense of ebbing and flowing life, and says, "I became absolutely convinced, beyond the shadow of a doubt, that this life element in me was indestructible, and that whatever happened to the body in which it had heretofore existed, it would survive and henceforth be imperishable." Then he makes a more striking statement still. He tells us that his bias was in favor of going on into the unknown rather than returning to natural life. It was only the remembrance of his family and friends, and loyalty to the efforts of the surgeon, that made him exert himself in a powerful wish to live. His physician afterward told him that his heart had been alarmingly affected, and that several times he (the physician) thought he was about to go. They both concluded that the heart action represented first the desire to slip away, and then the powerful effort to remain living. He says, "The absolute certainty that death was not the end but merely a new beginning, was pre-eminent in my mind." He says another thing which will be of interest to us: "Had I lived a blameless moral life, which I had not, I could not have felt less remorse for the past. There was no regret for lost opportunities, no reviewing of life's history, no concern whatever for reward or punishment, only a strong abiding sense of calmness and peace, and that I was in the hands of an infinitely benign Power which cared for me and would protect me from all that was ill; a Power whose attributes were goodness and mercy. The whole scheme of life on this earth, death, and the certain life to come, seemed to have meaning and purpose, to be harmonious, natural, and, above all, beneficent."

That is a piece of disinterested evidence which is worth a very great deal. May I add to that another piece of evidence, from a nurse who had charge of a very difficult, bad-tempered, and irreligious patient, whom we will call Mrs. X. There is not space here to give the whole story, but I will summarize it. The patient had given a great deal of trouble, and when she felt the approach of death, said, very angrily: "Why should I have to die? So-and-so does not keep her house nearly as clean as I do. I have taken care of my husband and little boy and kept my house clean, why should I die? I call it cruel of God. And I don't want anybody to say any prayers, and I won't see the vicar, not if he comes ever so much, I won't." The nurse said: "I did not know what to do. My heart ached for her." Then the patient died. The nurse writes, "I will not dwell upon the symptoms of death. They were all present. I closed the eyelids, straightened her hands across her breast, put the sheets tidy and turned to the open window. I stayed there two or three minutes. When I returned to the bed I saw a faint quiver in a muscle of the throat. I told myself that it was nothing, but in another moment there was a tremor of the lips. Horrified, I put a spoon with some brandy into the mouth of Mrs. X. She opened her eyes and said slowly, in a voice I had never heard before, and solemn beyond description, "I have been dead and I am alive again." Then she paused and added: "But all my dying's done. I have seen the angels, two of them by our apple tree, more beautiful than I can tell." The nurse added,

"This was the more amazing because Mrs. X had no belief in angels nor any hope of a further life at all." The nurse gave her some medicine, and after she had drunk it she said, "I am always going to do what they want." When the doctor came in she repeated the same words and he laughed at her and said she had never been dead. She said to him: "Don't laugh. It is all true. I have seen the angels and all my dying's done." The nurse added, "When the spirit really left the body twenty-four hours later, it was like the gentlest falling asleep of a little child."

Curiously enough, that nurse, afterward, went very near death herself. She said, "I heard the doctor saying to another nurse, 'Can you still feel the pulse, nurse?' and his voice sounded far off and of no consequence. Then he spoke louder and asked me to rouse myself, and I heard my own voice answer, 'No, I don't want to.' I was with my father, who had been dead some years, and I had seen the face of my dear brother who was drowned when I was a little girl, but alas! the gates had closed against me and I had to come back." I want the reader to notice the word "alas."

Nor does the evidence of the specialist conflict with this. The famous specialist, Sir H. Thompson, says, "I venture to state as a known result of long and careful observation of the phenomena which occur at the close of life, that a really painful death from disease is rarely witnessed." Sir Frederick Treves, at one time the King's physician, says in his reminiscences, "What is termed the 'agony of death' concerns the watcher by the bedside rather than the being who is the subject of pity. The last illness may be long, wearisome, and painful, but the closing moments of it are free from suffering. Where there appears to be a terrible struggle the subject is unconscious of it. It is the onlooker who bears the misery of it; to the subject there is merely a moment,

> 'When something like a white wave of the sea
> Breaks o'er the brain and buries us in sleep.'"

After all, is not this exactly what we should expect? For death is the ordinance of God. Not an untimely death, but death at some time or another is the will of God. Sometimes it is hastened by human folly, ignorance, or sin; but it differs from suffering in that many people go through life with little or no physical suffering, but no one escapes death.

Imagine now, for a moment, the unborn babe within his mother's womb. If he had the power to contemplate the life into which he was going to enter, would he not be terrified? In that prenatal life he is warm and cosy and nourished, without effort of his own. What a terrible, cold, friendless place this world would appear, could he dream of it, and how he would dread the process of birth! Yet how beautifully God has arranged that process, for when the baby is first conscious of anything his head is pillowed on his mother's breast, his nourishment is only a few inches away from his mouth, there are arms which hold him very tightly and there are eyes which smile lovingly into his own. If God guards so carefully our entry into this world, will he be careless of our entry into another? Will he not know that we are frightened and timid and lonely, and will he not have taken care that the experience should be beautiful?

Indeed, I think the other life is so wonderful that we

have no faculties with which to assess or describe it. Can you imagine yourself rushing in from some glorious sunset and trying to describe it to a man born blind? "It is scarlet and yellow and gold," you say. But the words have no meaning to him. "Scarlet?" he says. "What's that?" You could only say it was like the blare of a trumpet; you could only describe the sense-impression he couldn't receive through one that he could. Yellow, you might say, is like the smell of a lily and gold is like the feel of silk. What sort of sunset would he imagine? We have no faculties to enter even imaginatively the wonders of another life. "Eye hath not seen, nor ear heard, neither have entered into the heart of man the things which God hath prepared for them that love Him."[2]

The analogy reminds me of a similar one used by Doctor Fosdick, and this links us up with the second part of our question, "How do we know that life goes on?" Doctor Fosdick imagines twin babes unborn within the mother, gifted with the power of thought, one a skeptic and the other a believer, and both living without light and without breathing. "The crisis of birth," he says, "tearing them loose from the matrix on which their existence seems fundamentally to depend would appear to them like death. As for picturing the world without it would be impossible. The skeptic babe would say to the believer: 'You want to go on living, and so you think you will, but that is not scientific. Existence depends on present circumstances and when those circumstances go, life goes also.' The believing babe would say: 'I believe there is something afterward. Nature has been at work developing some things that have no meaning here, and nature is not irra-

[2] 1 Corinthians 2. 9.

tional. We cannot picture the new life, but I am confident that nature is not so senseless to undertake such a promising process with no end in view.' "

So, just as the child within the womb might argue—with unimaginable precocity—that eyes and lips and ears involved seeing and tasting and hearing, so man not only finds within himself a passionate desire for more and fuller life, but believes he has powers, latent within him, which can only be expressed in a life wider than this. He craves a world where justice is done, where righteousness triumphs, where loved ones are rejoined. Unless nature is irrational even his power to dream of an immortal life is some kind of argument for its probability.

The alternative is that this splendid achievement of nature which we call man (man who would fiercely deny that he is no greater than any other form of organic life), can be pushed out of existence by a germ so small that a million can sit on the head of a pin. The whole rationality of nature is impeached if nature's final consummation can be utterly annihilated by, say, a fall of coal, or an exploding shell, or a surgeon's mistake.

But, says the skeptic, what is your answer to the view that when the brain dies we end our lives completely? This you will remember was the argument of Sir Arthur Keith, who used the illustration of a candle (though it is very dangerous to argue from analogies), and said that when the candle is done, the flame goes out and when the body is done (and the brain is part of the body) the soul is extinguished. In his book *Phantom Walls,* Sir Oliver Lodge says:[3] "The image or illustration is quite a good one; but Sir Arthur did not follow it up as a physicist

[3] Page 52.

would. He limited himself to the material particles of the candle, and to the perceptible flame, just as an anatomist would. He did not bethink himself of what was happening in space. The candle was not lighted without an object. Its object was to illuminate something, that is to say, to emit light. And what is light? Not something in the candle, but something which emanates from the candle and goes away into space; something different from matter, though associated with it. The real function of a candle depends on the properties of space; it is emitting something into space which, if space is free and empty of matter, will go on forever. Just as we see the light of a distant star or a nebulous cloud which has been traveling for eight hundred thousand years before it reaches our eye—for that is how we see, for instance, the great nebula in Andromeda, quite visible to the naked eye on a dark night, we see it as it was eight hundred thousand years ago—so an observer, with a sufficiently sensitive instrument, could detect the light of the Armada beacons still. Therefore I say the illustration is a good one; and suggests, rather than negatives, the immortality of the soul."[4]

I am rather fond of another kind of analogy. I imagine a man who is dumb but who is a very beautiful violinist. Imagine that he cannot speak in words or even in signs; that he can only play the violin. His violin is his only means of manifestation to the outer world. Now, imagine that the violin represents a man's body which includes his brain, and that the man represents the soul. You will then perceive what the old philosopher meant when he said: "It is not true to say man is a body and has a soul.

[4] Page 58.

It is true to say man is a soul and has a body." At present we are like the man with the violin. He can only express himself through it. Apart from things like telepathy, which we will leave out of our survey for the moment, our body is our only means of manifesting ourselves in the world. In order to convey a message to other people I must use some part of my body, my fist, or my voice, or my eyes, and so on.

But supposing, in our illustration, that somebody smashes the man's violin. Why should we suppose that the man himself is damaged? What is to prevent him finding some other instrument which he can play? And why should we suppose that when a man's body is smashed up or his brain injured or destroyed, that he does not go on and find some other means of manifestation? The illustration goes further. If a violin is damaged, then it may be that only squeaks can be drawn from it, but the man remains untouched behind it. So in the case of our friends who suffer the mental illness we call insanity. They cannot make contact with us in a normal way, but they themselves are not idiots; it is only that they have either inherited or developed a damaged violin. A player is distinct from a faulty instrument.

For the philosophically minded I would say that this is in harmony with the philosophic theory most widely held at the moment. No philosopher identifies the brain with the personality. The three common theories are epiphenomenalism, parallelism, and interactionism. The first thinks of consciousness as an epiphenomenon, something thrown off by the brain in the course of its activities, but not the purpose of its activities. The best illustration I know is that of sparks given off by the wheels of an engine as it chafes the rails. The second theory, parallelism, suggests that every activity of the brain carries with it a parallel activity in consciousness, and vice versa. But that does not decide which is cause and which is effect. The third theory, interactionism, is the one held by most philosophers; that the brain and the mind are certainly linked together at present; that the two are interlocked in an extraordinary way, but that no one knows what is the relationship between them.

Certainly, no thinker would identify mind and brain. When you say "I," you don't mean your brain any more than you mean your fist. You use your brain with which to think. As a matter of fact, not a particle remains today of the brain you had twenty years ago, and yet you would admit that the things done twenty years ago were done by you, and that if there is either praise or blame it must be charged up to you. If a man, therefore, says "How can I go on when my brain is finished?" it is interesting to answer, "But you have had a dozen brains and you are still going on." The brain may be the instrument of our thinking, and, if you like, even of our loving, but it is certainly not the source of either. Nobody who has ever seen a human brain on the dissecting table can really believe that that white pulpy mass, as much like sweetbread as anything, can, of itself, produce poems and symphonies and all the glories of art and literature and love.

Pass to another piece of evidence which can be expressed quite simply and briefly. Either God is a devil or he is good, or he is incapable of managing his universe. In other words, he is either bad, good, or stupid. I cannot at this point take time to think those three lines out very carefully or fully. If you are going to say he is evil.

there are certain things that might seem to support your theory. But I cannot myself believe that behind lovely flowers, and a child's laughter, and a woman's love, and Chopin's music, and Turner's paintings, and Browning's poetry, and deeds like Oates's, when that very gallant gentleman went out into the blizzard to die—is not holiness but a leering obscenity. I find it equally hard to believe that God is stupid, that he has made a universe which has run away with him. I agree that when he gave men free will he opened the door to disharmony in his universe, and many things happen which are not his will and which, for the moment, he cannot help. But ultimately I believe he is omnipotent, and those who are tempted to think that he is stupid and defeated had better read one book by Sir James Jeans and ask themselves whether this universe was made by a fool. The alternative, then, is love, and I wish to put before the skeptic this picture.

I can remember, as though it were yesterday, standing in a little front parlor of a home in Leeds. The blinds were drawn down. The dim light shone through them. A broken-hearted mother and father were standing with me beside the coffin of their little child. I can remember now how the light between the edge of the blind and the window frame drew the gold from his curly head as he lay before us with a half-smile upon his marble face. I believe that behind the shadows there was a Face, infinitely tender and kind, and a voice that would fain have said to us all: "Suffer it to be so now. It is part of the burden of the world's ignorance or folly or sin. You shall hold him again in your arms, and come at last to see that nothing precious is lost." That is what the three of us believed as we stood there. Do you believe that behind the shadows there was the leering of a fiend, laughing behind his hand at our fond delusion? Or do you believe that behind the shadows was the gummy, senseless, slavering face of some immensely powerful imbecile? The only other alternative is that of love and power and invincible purpose. The second point in the evidence for immortality, then, is the nature and character of God.

The third piece of evidence is that of Jesus; not, I think, evidence of his resurrection, for it is not safe to argue that because something happens to a unique person it will happen to us; though that great fact does help. Someone, and Someone human, has broken the barrier between death and life. That is immensely strong supporting evidence, but of itself not sufficient to prove our survival. But the evidence of Jesus which helps me most is his own certainty. He is so certain that he does not attempt to prove. He does what, in his case, is more convincing. He takes immortality for granted. I will take only one instance where several could be taken. In the last dread hour a dying thief hangs on the cross next his own. A dying *thief*. Not one of the elect; not one supposed to have qualified for a reward hereafter. And this poor, smitten wretch cries out to Jesus, hardly knowing what his words mean, "Lord, remember me when thou comest into thy kingdom." Now note the answer of Jesus carefully. "This day you shall be with me in the world of spirits." There is no argument, "If you are good and repent, you shall go to heaven." What is much more impressive for our present purpose is this. Jesus does not say, "I hope so." He says, "You shall be there." Now, either Jesus was sure or he was not sure. If he were not sure, he would have said, "Well, I hope we shall meet again," or, "It is my faith that we shall pass on to another life." Either, then, he *knew* or he was not honest. I challenge the skeptic with that.

And I imagine the skeptic turns now, and says, "But how did he know?" Forget for the moment all your theology about the person of Christ, and look at it for one moment like this: You and I are standing with Turner facing a picture. Turner is criticizing the picture. To you he says: "Yes, it is a very good picture indeed. There is just that one tint that is too strong, or there is just that one line that is not true." And you turn to me and say, "How does he know?" I reply to you, "Know? Surely, Turner knows what is good in a picture. If not, no one knows. He is the master. This is his subject." You and I are standing with Chopin listening while someone plays. When the music is finished Chopin says to us, "Very good, but the full beauty is not brought out when it is played so fast, and at one point he played a discord." And you turn to me and say, "How does he know?" My reply is the same: "Know when there is a discord—Chopin?" We stand together with Shakespeare, who is criticizing a sonnet, and as he puts it down he says: "That is not a sonnet at all. This is wrong and that is wrong." You say to me, "How does he know?" and I reply, "If he doesn't know, nobody does." I have only to mention the name "Shakespeare" and you need no other evidence. The master is speaking on his own subject.

Forget, for the moment, all your theories about the person of Jesus. Is he a great religious genius or not? I do not ask you to take Shakespeare's opinions on sermons, but I do on sonnets. I do not ask you to agree with

Turner if he speaks on politics, but I do on paintings. I do not demand that you should agree with Chopin on mushrooms, but I do on music. And if you like to prove to me that Jesus Christ made mistakes in his science or regarding the authorship of a psalm, I shall not turn a hair. A person who lived in Galilee two thousand years ago and knew all modern science would have been a monstrosity, not a perfect man. But when he is talking about religion, do you think he had not got the evidence; do you think he had not contemplated all the possible adventures in the history of the soul? Had not that amazing mind contemplated all the mysteries of life and death? Did he know? If *he* does not know, nobody does. A perfect man can know God and trust God in any age. But some of us have thought, and thought, and thought, and are forced to a further conclusion, that the eyes that on that dreadful day were turned in love and compassion toward the dying thief were the eyes of God, and that whenever the Master spoke about his own subject, which was religion, he revealed the eternal truth of God.

He could not tell us much. For we could not understand. We are fools and blind, and what bit of vision we have is clouded with sin. But he lays a cool hand on fevered spirit and tortured body and frenzied brain. His quiet eyes hold our agony and silence its outcry. He whispers that God is love and all is well, and there is in his voice, no false comfort, no shallow optimism, or easy lie. He himself has tasted death and qualified in the world's dread school of pain. He cannot tell us much. We could not bear it. But when he says that the final meaning of life is love, and a love which ultimately wins without the annihilation of one, without the loss of the free will of one, without the loss of the intellectual integrity of one, we find ourselves believing him, for truth was the very air his soul breathed. "Why," he says, "if it were not so, I would have told you."

So, my friend, be of good cheer! When the long day is over, you will walk in the scented dusk down the last valley; and not alone, for he, the Companion of all men, has pledged his word to be with you. And at the end of that valley, all hushed and quiet, "By velvet darkness folded in," you will see, shining through the trees, the lights of home. One evening the lamps will be lighted for you in the House of New Beginnings. And when you draw near to the house, you will hear music and dancing.